Stand in Truth

Live in the Freedom of Judgment

Jaclyn Palmer

Inseparable Ministries Inc Publishing
Meridian, Idaho
2023

Stand in Truth

Live in the Freedom of Judgment

First Printing, 2023

ISBN 979-8-9879788-0-1

Cover design: Linda Boatman, painting by Jaclyn Palmer
Edited: skillfully by Carolyn Coburn Tragesser
Proofread: Kelly Murray

Published in the United States of America
Inseparable Ministries Inc Publishing
1200 N Main Street
Meridian, Idaho
www.womeninseparable.com

Dedication

To those girls who sat with me
at the start of this journey.
Coffee poured. Scripture opened.
Conversation and laughter etched.
&
To my Jesus, always.

Table of Contents

Introduction

About This Study

As we begin this journey through the book of 1 Corinthians, I encourage you to do two things: First, participate in the truth that Paul presented to the Corinthian body of believers by taking the truth of his words to heart in a personal way. Second, remember that you are not a Corinthian believer. You are not walking in their city or in their church or in their shoes. This letter is a personal response to the matters that were infesting their unity as a Christian community. Paul's words are both personal to the Corinthians and universal to the family of God. Once we learn how to differentiate the two, then Truth will rain upon each of us unifying us as individuals designed by the Creator.

The Corinthian fail happened when judgment among themselves bred contention that shifted their eyes off Christ and onto each other. Paul desired they turn their eyes back to Christ by focusing on theology rather than preference. By doing so, the Christians of Corinth were free to be the individuals they were — individuals crafted by God, loved by Jesus Christ, filled with the Holy Spirit, and members of the Christian body.

Throughout this study, we will read Paul's response to their inquisitions. To begin, however, I would like to follow Paul's path and remember who the body of Christ is before approaching the sins and questions that were weighing them down. *"To the church of God that is in Corinth, to those sanctified in Christ Jesus, called to be saints."* (1 Corinthians 1:2) You are, he reminds the Corinthians, now part of the Church; no longer attending a building but are now a member of the body of God. You are freely set apart (sanctified) from your former ways, your past religion, and your old behaviors. You are now saints of the Living God: alive for Him!

1

Scripture Format

You will find a chapter of 1 Corinthians inserted at the start of each chapter in this book. I followed the format of Crossway's ESV Reader's Bible by removing all verse numbers from the text. This puts it back into its original intent as a letter rather than the chapter and verse so graciously included in our modern Bibles, 1227 AD. May I encourage you to pause and read Paul's letter before and after you read our study of his letter, chapter by chapter?

Throughout each chapter, you will see each Scripture inserted in a particular fashion for a specific reason. A college professor encouraged me once upon a time to write out Scripture one part at a time. In doing this, we easily see the intent of each word and can sweetly allow it to mold itself into our brain and into our heart. To hide His Word in our heart is an ever-challenging quest for those who trust in Christ. May this Scripture format aid your personal goal to see Scripture for what it is—a personal communication between you and God. May we purpose to take it in, word by word, and witness its fruit in our lives.

About Paul

Either you like him, or you do not. It is true. Ask around. Some will stand beside him with pure admiration; others will turn their heads with a slight gesture of, "I know God used him, but I am not particularly sold." I have gone back and forth. More back, I fear, than forth. I viewed him as a "say it like it is" kind of guy minus love, yet he is the author of the very book known for the famous chapter of love. With that said, if the author of this book is an author of love, then why did I feel so judged by his words?

I would love to know what you know about Paul. What comes to mind when you hear his name? A word, thought, or story? Do your thoughts begin with his upbringing as a student of the renowned Jewish Rabbi, Gamaliel? (Acts 5:34; 22:3) Do they begin with his initiating and observing the execution of Stephen? (Acts 7:54–8:3) Do you find yourself on the road to Damascus seeing Paul stumble about blinded by the Bright Light that overtook his pathway, hearing the words spoken to his heart by God above? (Acts 9:1–9) I wonder how many of us began our thoughts on Paul by remembering that his name was Saul. We recall the fearsome reputation Saul had in the Christian community. And then I wonder, how many of us smile as we remember that one day Saul believed in the very Name he lived to despise (Acts 9:17–20), and from that point on until his death, Saul had a new reputation and a new name! (Acts 13:9)

Some of us noted that he was the greatest missionary in our Christian history. That he penned the most books of our New Testament, or we considered the physical sufferings that he faithfully endured for the glorifying of the name of Jesus Christ (2 Corinthians 11:24–27). Regardless of what we knew — or just learned — the truth is, Paul was an outstanding man of intellect, of strength, of determination, and of endurance. Paul had a passion and a purpose. His passion was his Savior, and his purpose was the same: to live for Jesus. His life was all for Jesus. So, whether we have a love or a "not liking so much" feeling toward this man and his words, we cannot deny his love for Jesus Christ.

About Sosthenes

My question is the same about this man as it was with Paul. What word, thought or story comes to mind when you hear his name? What do you know about this co-laborer of Paul? Some stare blankly at the oh-so-foreign name of Sosthenes. Some are smiling and penning their knowledge and admiration, while others of us are quickly scanning our mental Bible attempting to locate any recollection of such an important individual as Sosthenes. Honestly, I never noticed his name until I sat intentionally with this letter. His recorded story is quite small, but the depth of his presence is amazing. His name is in Scripture only twice (1 Corinthians 1:1 and Acts 18:17), yet his name is sealed in the Lamb's Book of Life for eternity.

And they all seized Sosthenes, the ruler of the synagogue, and beat him in front of the tribunal. But Gallio paid no attention to any of this.
Acts 18:17; circa. 60 A.D

3

Paul, called by the will of God to be an apostle of Christ Jesus,
and our brother Sosthenes,
1 Corinthians 1:1; circa. 65 A.D

I encourage you to do as I have recently done, read these verses as if they are regarding a respectable man you know on a personal level. Make Sosthenes' story real. Take it to heart and appreciate who he was in the eyes of the Lord.

Here's his story. Claudius, the emperor of Rome, had commanded all Jews to leave the area. Two of the Jews who left due to this law were Paul's friends Aquila and Priscilla. At this time, Paul traveled to Corinth to visit and stay with them for a year and a half. While there, he weekly frequented the synagogue to persuade Jews and Greeks toward the love of Jesus Christ in place of the law of Moses. The Greeks were seeing the truth, but some Jews held on to their roots. Finally, Paul "shook his garments"[1] to the Jews and retreated to a friend's house who, coincidentally, lived next door to the synagogue.

Crispus, the ruler of the Jewish synagogue (next door), was at Titius' house with Paul, because he was a believer of Jesus of Nazareth was Christ, the prophesied Son of God. Ultimately, church was happening right next door to the holy synagogue! Along with Crispus and his family, natives of the city were gathering in Titius Justus' house to worship Jesus Christ. How magnificent!

However, unbelieving Jews brought Paul before Gallio, the city council, to silence him saying, "This man is persuading people to worship God contrary to the law." (v.12) Gallio replied, "This is a matter between you and your own law. I refuse to judge these things." Then he kicked Paul and the Jews out of his court. In the street outside of the courthouse, the Greeks seized Sosthenes, Crispus' replacement as ruler of the Jewish Synagogue, and beat him. Gallio had little interest in the matter.[2]

---

[1] Acts 18:6; Matthew 10:14 (5–15)
[2] Acts 18:17

Days later, Paul left the city of Corinth. The account of Sosthenes begins and ends in Acts 18, until Paul sits to respond to a letter he received from the Christian body of Corinth. As Paul sits to write, Sosthenes pulls up a chair joining in the role of authorship. Would you not love to know what happened in Sosthenes' heart from the public beating to his companionship with the Apostle Paul?

About Corinth

This is where my problem began with 1 Corinthians. I took the harshness of Paul's statements, forgetting that I am not in trouble. I read these in modern-day Christianity for the intent of learning from someone else's wrongdoing and corrections. May I take this book to heart? Most definitely! But the urgency in which Paul speaks is in response to a church seeking his counsel. You see, this city was a tough place to learn the newness of a Christian life: to be fully His. The ways of the city were still present in the church.

> *Corinth became so notorious for its evils that the term Korinthiazomai ("to act like a Corinthian") became a synonym for debauchery and prostitution.[3]*

The people of this church knew Paul. Personally. Paul started this church with a sweet handful of men and women who believed. (Acts 17:15–34) After his time in Corinth, he departed to continue building churches and teaching believers. During this time, Paul was receiving letters of concern and questions seeking his counsel for spiritual and scandalous situations. Therefore, Paul wrote this extensive letter to the Corinthian Church. At the time of Paul's written response to these inquiries, he was closing a three-year residence in Ephesus.

> *No letter in the New Testament deals so forcibly with local church problems, and perhaps no New Testament letter is more neglected today.[4]*

---

[3] Wilkinson and Boa, *Talk Thru the Bible* (Nashville; Thomas Nelson, 1983), 381
[4] Warren W. Wiersbe, *Wiersbe's Expository Outlines on the New Testament* (Colorado; Chariot Victor), 417

With boldness and passion, he addresses his response to his converts and fellow believers at Corinth. Paul receives reports of sin, disputes, and questions regarding Christian conduct.

Can you see this new family of God? Each week somebody new walks in. Before him sits a diverse crowd of individuals. Some have the smoke of paganism on their hardened faces; some have the appearance still wrapped around them as they sit in their air of leftover legalism. All trying to figure out how to transition into this new way of freedom in Christ. You can see why there were questions and confusion, and why they so easily judged one another.

In the midst of those people attempting to conquer their past religious experiences, entered those who were Corinthians, born and bred. How easy is it for one, scarred by the world, to "fit in" with those scarred by religion? Put that way, judgment makes sense. It is human nature, instinct. As you and I are picturing it, we are seeing our reality and battling thoughts of stereotypes and judging it all.

Being from Las Vegas, I get this. Corinth makes sense to me. I see the normalcy of the heartache that built up the city into what it is. Corinth, like Vegas, was a city known for its allowance and acceptance of outward sin. Actionable sins were on the street corners, in the public squares, and in the churches. Its enticement to visit drew you in, then bid you farewell with a taste of regret.

About Chloe

Is there a greater gift than a woman who calls you out? Okay, perhaps I should reword that. I should say, is there a greater gift than a friend who speaks life into you? Yes, that is better. Friend, meet Chloe. I wish Paul and Sosthenes had taken a quick minute to describe Chloe to us. That is not too much to ask for. How beautiful to know how she styled her hair on a Tuesday, her favorite pastimes, or her greatest dreams.

We may not know Chloe's physical details of height, weight, wrinkles, season of life, or passions. But we do know she was a brave woman who desired truth at the risk of her own acceptance. The Corinthian believers were learning how to be Christians without the rituals of paganism or the laws of legalism. How hard it is to learn to walk in freedom! This body of Christ did not have the written Word of God to glean knowledge. They had one another. They had Paul, and they sought Paul for all their wonderings. Paul explained to them the power and personal presence of the Holy Spirit, yet he was truly their only tangible source of Truth.

So, they wrote to Paul. And Paul wrote to the Corinthians. Correspondence between Paul and the new believers is where spiritual truth grew. We do not know the number of letters Chloe wrote, but we do know she penned at least one tough one. She saw the division that was taking place among her friends. She heard the arguments. She felt the emotions of dissension. She took all that she saw, heard, and felt and wrote a letter in search of clarification.

> *For it has been reported to me by Chloe's people*
> *that there is quarreling among you, my brothers.*
> *1 Corinthians 1:11*

About Jesus

Jesus was there when the beauty of Genesis 1 was spoken into existence, for He is the eternal Son of God. Yet, He desired to become man so He could fully relate with you and me. In doing so, Jesus came to this world as a human; in the form of a baby, raised as a child, experienced the struggles of humanity. Jesus desired to embrace human affection, to feel sorrow, to develop lasting relationships, and to understand the sting of betrayal by those closest to him. He chose to know, relate, and understand.

He did this out of love. Love is always best demonstrated rather than stated. Jesus expressed God's love to us in the clearest way imaginable, through life. He came to demonstrate God's love by relating to our humanity. And gracious, we could all testify that being a human is not always the easiest thing to be!

Never before has a religious leader or founder ever conquered death. When a person dies, regardless of how much peace they proclaim, that is it. All opportunities to state or demonstrate love are over. No one can conquer death.

But Jesus was not a religious founder; Jesus is the Son of God!

Psalm 19 declares the cries of worship that pour forth from all of creation: the sun, moon, stars, mountains, and rocks. He created everything all for His glory.

Yet only one creation received the ability to proclaim the name of Jesus Christ. When Jesus Christ rose from the grave—conquering sin, death, and eternal separation from God—He offered you a relationship with God Almighty. God gave you the gift of Eternal Salvation. As a child of God through the love of Jesus Christ, we have the opportunity to demonstrate our love for Him through living and proclaiming and shining forth His Light.

Friend, if you are meeting Jesus for the first time, will you pause for a moment to look at these truths in a Bible? You can easily access the free YouVersion app if you do not have a tangible Bible near you.

- Jesus is the Son of God: John 14
- Jesus lived for me: John 1
- Jesus died for me: Matthew 27
- Jesus rose again for me: Matthew 28
- Jesus is praying for me: John 17
- Jesus holds my future: Revelation 21

"Because, if you confess with your mouth that Jesus is Lord and believe in your heart that God raised him from the dead, you will be saved. For with the heart one believes and is justified, and with the mouth one confesses and is saved. For everyone who calls on the name of the Lord will be saved."
Romans 10:9–10, 13

1 Corinthians 1

Paul, called by the will of God to be an apostle
of Christ Jesus, and our brother Sosthenes,

To the church of God that is in Corinth, to those sanctified in Christ Jesus,
called to be saints together with all those who in every place call upon
the name of our Lord Jesus Christ, both their Lord and ours: Grace
to you and peace from God our Father and the Lord Jesus Christ.

I give thanks to my God always for you because of the grace of God that was
given you in Christ Jesus, that in every way you were enriched in him in
all speech and all knowledge — even as the testimony about Christ was
confirmed among you — so that you are not lacking in any gift, as you wait
for the revealing of our Lord Jesus Christ, who will sustain you to the end,
guiltless in the day of our Lord Jesus Christ. God is faithful, by whom
you were called into the fellowship of his Son, Jesus Christ our Lord.

I appeal to you, brothers, by the name of our Lord Jesus Christ, that all of you
agree, and that there be no divisions among you, but that you be united in
the same mind and the same judgment. For it has been reported to me by
Chloe's people that there is quarreling among you, my brothers. What I mean
is that each one of you says, "I follow Paul," or "I follow Apollos," or "I follow
Cephas," or "I follow Christ." Is Christ divided? Was Paul crucified for you?
Or were you baptized in the name of Paul? I thank God that I baptized none
of you except Crispus and Gaius, so that no one may say that you were
baptized in my name. (I did baptize also the household of Stephanas. Beyond
that, I do not know whether I baptized anyone else.) For Christ did not
send me to baptize but to preach the gospel, and not with words of
eloquent wisdom, lest the cross of Christ be emptied of its power.

For the word of the cross is folly to those who are perishing, but to us who are being saved it is the power of God. For it is written, "I will destroy the wisdom of the wise, and the discernment of the discerning I will thwart."

Where is the one who is wise? Where is the scribe? Where is the debater of this age? Has not God made foolish the wisdom of the world? For since, in the wisdom of God, the world did not know God through wisdom, it pleased God through the folly of what we preach to save those who believe. For Jews demand signs and Greeks seek wisdom, but we preach Christ crucified, a stumbling block to Jews and folly to Gentiles, but to those who are called, both Jews and Greeks, Christ the power of God and the wisdom of God. For the foolishness of God is wiser than men, and the weakness of God is stronger than men.

For consider your calling, brothers: not many of you were wise according to worldly standards, not many were powerful, not many were of noble birth. But God chose what is foolish in the world to shame the wise; God chose what is weak in the world to shame the strong; God chose what is low and despised in the world, even things that are not, to bring to nothing things that are, so that no human being might boast in the presence of God. And because of him you are in Christ Jesus, who became to us wisdom from God, righteousness and sanctification and redemption, so that, as it is written, "Let the one who boasts, boast in the Lord."

1

You Are His

I appeal to you, brothers,
by the name of our Lord Jesus Christ,
that all of you agree,
and that there be no divisions among you,
but that you be united
in the same mind and the same judgment.
1 Corinthians 1:10

May I set out a basket? I hope it will be a small one but setting out a basket is necessary. Here is my request as you enter this study: Will you drop a rock into our beloved basket? You can label it or drop it in anonymously. You can cling to it if so desired. I certainly do at times. Feel free to shove your rock in your pocket or cute handbag. Again, I certainly have. In fact, when starting this journey through the letter to the Corinthians, I had a basket of stones decorating my desk, a few scattered at my feet, and a couple propped beside my keyboard—just in case.

Judgment is a real battle—one that happens easily and frequently. Not necessarily because we are innately horrible people, but because we are alive, and we are human. So, yes to the innate trait. But this is not okay.

Sin nature cannot surpass the love of God in us. It cannot. If we can stand before God in the presence of Jesus Christ as the Holy Spirit fills us, then our hands and hearts ought not have room enough for these stones of judgment.

Let me be clear. There is a vast variety of stone throwing judgments out there. We have experienced stones from the words of those around us. These stones hurt. They hurt every time. Words spoken to us tend to live deep within us causing us to remember them repeatedly. Words saying that you are not good enough. You are not capable, worthy, or wanted. These stones hurt. I am sorry for the words that have rooted themselves in you. I am sorry for the anger, sorrow, self-doubt and hurt these words birth within you. I am sorry, and I understand.

Let us also consider stones that we throw at others. We do, don't we? As I pen these words, our world is facing a challenge. A pandemic entered societies from ocean to ocean. Fear and anxiety, skepticism and hatred — stones upon stones hurled across country lines, across city lines, in grocery stores, in our churches, at our authority, and even at our dearest of people. It is as if this pandemic has shattered each of us at our very core. We do not know how to process this ever-shifting society, so we throw.

Lastly, there are those stones we unearth from our past, that emerge from our guilt, from our shame, from the mirror, from social media, from comparison, from deep within…. By repeatedly targeting ourselves with such, we cause unnecessary pain in our own thoughts and hearts. In place of defending ourselves against the judgment of others, we accept the judgment and brutalize our soul worse than anyone could ever imagine. This I know, for I am highly guilty of this unruly crime.

We must acknowledge the repetition of this cyclical display of ungodliness. As we journey through this difficult letter by the Apostle Paul to the church family spread throughout the city of Corinth, we will quickly identify with the carnage of judgment. For this reason, I suggest trying to drop your stones before entering in. Or sit with me as I ease my fingers free, little by little.

Scripture:

Grace to you and peace from God our Father and the Lord Jesus Christ.
1 Corinthians 1:3

The introduction chapter details Bible references about Paul and Sosthenes. If you have not read that yet (no judgment for jumping ahead), I do encourage you to revisit that chapter when your time and interest allows. As a non-fan of Paul, I must confess that I have turned tail on my opinion of this man as I studied the book of 1 Corinthians. I am not lying when I say, "I had a basket of stones decorating my desk, a few scattered at my feet, and a couple propped beside my keyboard just in case." I etched my stones with preconceived notions of this man and his letter to Corinth. I held those stones so tightly, I almost bled at times.

My thoughts of Paul were subpar, and my enticement to this book was nonexistent.

Perhaps you are with me on this platform, perhaps you are judging me for judging Paul, perhaps you have no idea what I am referring to. In any case, allow me to begin this next segment as pursued in the beginning of 1 Corinthians.

Jesus.

Jesus Christ is the changer of all matter. He changed the course of our future with His love. God spoke a word and brought matter into existence. Jesus Christ loved the human creation so dearly that He took on the form of humanity, walked, talked, lived, and engaged with all emotions and realities of the human race. He shed his blood, gave his life, and buried the cause of eternal separation of man from God. Jesus Christ rose from the grave giving new life to every soul, every story, every pain, and every sorrow. He is alive and living, once again, in the Heavenly realm. And Jesus Christ, the changer of all matter, is praying for you.[5]

---

[5] John 17

13

I would like for you and me to follow Paul's path in remembering who the body of Christ is before approaching the sins and questions that weighed the Corinthians down. You are, he reminds us all, the body of Christ. You are now part of the Church, no longer just attending in a building but are now a member of the body of God. You are free from your former ways, your past religion, and your old behaviors. You are now saints of the Living God, alive for Him!

He proceeds to charge these hungry hearts with a most beautiful discourse that makes me wonder how this is not a frequented conversation today. I understand our speech has altered just a bit, and our eloquence has found its form via an emoticon, but can you feel the smile on your heart if someone spoke these words to you in one modern way or another? Listen to what Paul has to say.

Scripture:

> Grace to you and peace from God our Father and the Lord Jesus Christ.
> I give thanks to my God always for you
> because of the grace of God that was given you in Christ Jesus,
> that in every way you were enriched in him
> in all speech and all knowledge —
> even as the testimony about Christ was confirmed among you —
> so that you are not lacking in any gift,
> as you wait for the revealing of our Lord Jesus Christ,
> who will sustain you to the end,
> guiltless in the day of our Lord Jesus Christ.
> God is faithful,
> by whom you were called into the fellowship of his Son,
> Jesus Christ our Lord.
> 1 Corinthians 1:3–9

As you read these words, do you find yourself standing a little taller? Are you a little surer of your purpose and true reputation? Do you desire to uphold this faithful saying as a sincere compliment of Christ's completion in you? Do you fall in love with Jesus just a touch more?

When you look at verses three to nine, you will find the name of Jesus Christ six times and God four times. The words found sprinkled around these names remind believers that they are followers of the Most-High God—that God fills them with His grace and gifts of knowledge and speech. They are the very testimony of God the Father made possible through the ultimate gift of love purchased by Jesus Christ's blood sacrifice on the cross. Because of whom they are in Him, they have hope — true hope. Not the "cross your fingers" kind of hope that leaves one restless but a hope, tried and true. A hope that is eternally secure, sure, and promised beyond measure. Hope in the very Creator and Sustainer of life itself.

Do you see what these six verses are about? They are all about Jesus. The Corinthian church had forgotten this truth. They had forgotten that Jesus is the answer, the way, the truth. Paul was eager to lead them back to Jesus Christ.

Have you been in their shoes? Have you swayed so far from Jesus that you do not even know where to begin to even look for Him? Friend, if you know Jesus Christ as your personal Savior, you are the daughter of the King of kings. Jesus' Word, the very Bible we are studying, is His promise for you. Neither your past nor present reality matters. It is about Jesus, and He is calling you into His open arms today.

No matter the situation, circumstance, heartache, or reality you are facing at this moment, He is there. He is faithful. He is true. He is your Father. He is your protector. He is your everything. And because He is your all in all, you are full of His strength, His truth, His love, and His forgiveness.

If you are sitting there wondering how you can overcome the matter at hand and "start fresh," allow me to encourage you to do two things:

- Pick up your Bible or Bible app and read one verse, perhaps two verses....
- Look at the Earth outside. Let the rocks, the sun, and the stars declare the Glory of the Lord.

For now, that is it. You do not need a big answer. You need Jesus, the ultimate answer. I have a feeling your next step(s) will come as you wade through the book of 1 Corinthians. When the time comes, your heart and eyes will be ready to proceed. For now, sit in wonder of God. Let His Word fill you and let all of creation proclaim His handiwork. Take this time to set your eyes on Jesus Christ by way of His written Word and His magnificent handiwork. Psalm 19:1–3 is a beautiful place to start.

The heavens declare the glory of God,
and the sky above proclaim his handiwork.
Day to day pours out speech,
and night to night reveals knowledge.
There is no speech, nor are there words,
whose voice is not heard.

Sit in the beauty of Jesus today. You may desire to take a moment to write out a verse that comforts your heart. You will find a place for notes at the end of each chapter to record any heart moment, thoughts, questions, and Scripture that you want to pursue for a later study.

Scripture:

I appeal to you, brothers,
by the name of our Lord Jesus Christ,
that all of you agree,
and that there be no divisions among you,
but that you be united
in the same mind and the same judgment.
For it has been reported to me
by Chloe's people that there is quarreling
among you, my brothers.
What I mean is that each one of you says,
"I follow Paul,"
or "I follow Apollos,"
or "I follow Cephas,"
or "I follow Christ."
Is Christ divided?

Was Paul crucified for you?
Or were you baptized in the name of Paul?
1 Corinthians 1:10–13

I appreciate Paul's approach to this matter of contention. He does not sit down and slowly take them through the conversations, attacks, and disputes that have unsettled this church body; he shoots at the main target. In doing so, he gains everyone's attention — and everyone's heart.

Paul exhorts the Corinthian church to stand against the allowance of contentions among them. Then he follows up saying, I know you have contentions among you. Chloe told me. And then he calls out the contention. Is Christ divided? The obvious answer is no. But the answer most justified within their hearts leans more toward an unspoken yes.

See if you can feel your way into this meeting.

Here you are sitting among church friends. Paul had written a letter to the church. All Corinthian believers are present.

You arrive and look around. You see familiar faces. You smile. Other faces, you quickly avoid. Hurrying to your seat, you hear someone reading Paul's letter from the front of the room. "Now I beseech you…by the name of our Lord Jesus Christ…." You can feel the silence, the smiles, and the peace overtake the congregation. The reader continues, "For it has been declared unto me…by Chloe…of contentions…." Heartrate and accusations conflict with the peace that was in your heart.

"Now I say that some of you say, I am of Paul. Some say, I am of Apollos. Some, I am of Cephas. Some, of Christ." Contentions arise in hearts throughout the room. You can feel your frustration increase. Then three simple words wash over each heart, "Is Christ divided?" "No," spoken in surprised agreement. It is the first thing agreed upon in some time. A seemingly blasphemous question then asked, "Was Paul crucified for you?" No. No, he was not. Just the thought sent chills of remorse down a few spines. Another question arises, "Were you baptized in the name of Paul?" No. No, but in the name of Jesus Christ!

17

Agreements shared among the hearts brought the first sign of light upon what has stirred up this level of contention. It is not about the man that led or started the group. Jesus Christ was the One crucified. Jesus Christ rose again. He alone washed us from our past, our sin. It is Jesus. Jesus.

Is it not heartbreaking how frequently contentions arise within our hearts, our groups, our churches, and within the very body of Christ?

Scripture:

> *I appeal to you, brothers,*
> *by the name of our Lord Jesus Christ,*
> *that all of you agree,*
> *and that there be no divisions among you,*
> *but that you be united*
> *in the same mind and the same judgment.*
> *1 Corinthians 1:10*

Speak the *same thing*. Be perfectly joined together in the *same mind* and in the *same judgment*. No divisions among you. Powerful. Beautiful.

Follow me here. Dispute was on the rise. The body of Christ was verbally abrasive one against the other. Chloe made Paul aware of this internal combustion. Something had to happen. An answer to the question had to be there. And, of course, there had to be a question asked to lead to the answer.

The question: What is the cause of contention? The answer: Shifted eyes.[6] The question: What is the resolution of contention? The answer: Shift your eyes. Contention solved. That simple? Yes. That simple.

Jude instructed and deeply encouraged us to "contend for the faith."[7] Paul tells us to "Put on the whole armor of God, that you may be able to

---

[6] Matthew 26:8
[7] Jude 3

stand against the schemes of the devil."[8] We are equipped to fight, and we are called to stand on the sure foundation of Jesus Christ, the One and only Savior.

But we are *not* to contend for the faith within the body of Christ! This is where the Corinthians failed. They entirely dropped the name of Jesus Christ and held on, rather, to the man who formed or led their group. Paul. Cephas (Peter). Apollos. Some did remain on the true foundation and claimed to be of Christ.

Are we not guilty of the same? I am. I am certainly guilty of casting my stones of preference and laws on the grace and liberty of Christ that another person, group, or church is embracing. And for that, I am sorry.

Jesus saved me. In Jesus, I am baptized. It is Jesus in whom I live for until the day He comes again. My epic failure, or shall we say, my Corinthian fail, flairs up each time I contend over my preferences rather than theology. And this is where the power and beauty of verse ten comes into play. We are to fight for the faith yet unite as the body of Christ.

Scripture:

> *I thank God that I baptized none of you…*
> *For Christ did not send me to baptize*
> *but to preach the gospel,*
> *and not with words of eloquent wisdom,*
> *lest the cross of Christ be emptied of its power.*
> *1 Corinthians 1:14a, 17*

Paul takes a step back to remind the Corinthians who he is. He was one man with one purpose: to preach the gospel. He reminded the followers that it is not about who baptized them, for baptism has nothing to do with the one who performs the baptism. Baptism is about identifying with Jesus' resurrection. Furthermore, he declares, I am not preaching my words but the gospel of Jesus Christ.

---

[8] Ephesians 6:11

He goes on for the next eight verses supporting his purpose of preaching the gospel. How perfect that he begins his letter to the Corinthian church calling out the contentions then declaring the purpose of preaching the gospel. You know what he is doing? He is refocusing their eyes.

Scripture:

> *Where is the one who is wise?*
> *Where is the scribe?*
> *Where is the debater of this age?*
> *Has not God made foolish the wisdom of the world?*
> *For since, in the wisdom of God,*
> *the world did not know God through wisdom,*
> *it pleased God through the folly*
> *of what we preach to save those who believe.*
> *For Jews demand signs and Greeks seek wisdom,*
> *but we preach Christ crucified,*
> *a stumbling block to Jews and folly to Gentiles,*
> *but to those who are called,*
> *both Jews and Greeks,*
> *Christ the power of God and the wisdom of God.*
> *For the foolishness of God is wiser than men,*
> *and the weakness of God is stronger than men.*
> *1 Corinthians 1:20–25*

This church had written to Paul regarding the rights and wrongs of Christian living. Paul had full intention of approaching each topic, hence the book of Corinthians, but first, he took a moment to refocus their eyes. He called them out, yes. But of the thirty-one verses in the first chapter, only eight of them are difficult to publicly swallow. The rest are all about Jesus Christ and the beauty of the gospel.

Paul says that God called him to preach — but not with his own words. I love that! God has called me to teach, but I am daily praying for His words. I, too, ought to refocus my eyes. For to me to teach is Christ. Words sell, yes. But Christ saves. Consider Billy Graham. Billy Graham is respectfully known as the most heard evangelist in history. His words were immensely simple. He preached the gospel. Period. Throughout America's social contentions and religious debates, Billy Graham was a man called by God to preach the gospel — and that is what he did.

Scripture:

> *And because of him you are in Christ Jesus,*
> *who became to us wisdom from God,*
> *righteousness and sanctification and redemption,*
> *so that, as it is written,*
> *'Let the one who boasts,*
> *boast in the Lord.*
> *1 Corinthians 1:30–31*

I sit here with these verses pondering who I am, what my calling is, and if I am using my platform for the sake of the gospel? Who are you? God has called you unto salvation. Are you using your daily platform for the sake of the gospel? Friend, as a child of God, you are sanctified by the name of Jesus Christ. Remember that. May we unite for the intent of growing in the theology that saves rather than the preferences that divide.

Jaclyn Palmer

Notes

1 Corinthians 2

*And I, when I came to you, brothers, did not come proclaiming to you
the testimony of God with lofty speech or wisdom. For I decided to know
nothing among you except Jesus Christ and him crucified. And I was
with you in weakness and in fear and much trembling, and my speech
and my message were not in plausible words of wisdom, but in
demonstration of the Spirit and of power, so that your faith might
not rest in the wisdom of men but in the power of God.*

*Yet among the mature we do impart wisdom, although it is not a wisdom
of this age or of the rulers of this age, who are doomed to pass away.
But we impart a secret and hidden wisdom of God, which God decreed before
the ages for our glory. None of the rulers of this age understood this, for if they
had, they would not have crucified the Lord of glory. But, as it is written,*

*"What no eye has seen, nor ear heard,
nor the heart of man imagined,
what God has prepared for those who love him" —*

*these things God has revealed to us through the Spirit. For the Spirit searches
everything, even the depths of God. For who knows a person's thoughts except
the spirit of that person, which is in him? So also no one comprehends
the thoughts of God except the Spirit of God. Now we have received not
the spirit of the world, but the Spirit who is from God, that we might
understand the things freely given us by God. And we impart this
in words not taught by human wisdom but taught by the Spirit,
interpreting spiritual truths to those who are spiritual.*

Jaclyn Palmer

The natural person does not accept the things of the Spirit of God, for they are folly to him, and he is not able to understand them because they are spiritually discerned. The spiritual person judges all things, but is himself to be judged by no one. "For who has understood the mind of the Lord so as to instruct him?" But we have the mind of Christ.

2

You Are Sealed

"For who has understood the mind of the Lord so as to instruct him?"
But we have the mind of Christ.
1 Corinthians 2:16

I did not graduate from high school. In fact, I never attended it. I could say the same thing about junior high. It was in my second-grade year that I was removed from the public-school system to be homeschooled. Starting in my third-grade year, books were ordered, but that was the extent of offered education. My family expected me to be self-taught and to take the initiative to accomplish unknown academic tasks. My education was far from sufficient, my grasp on basic academic knowledge far from ideal.

My mother led me to the Lord when I was three. I began learning and memorizing Scripture as young as I can remember. God the Father was very real to me. His arms were my favorite place of comfort and strength.

Academic knowledge proved to be minimal, yet wisdom was forever at my fingertips. How desperately I desired both.

One day, my junior high Sunday School teacher encouraged me to read the book of Proverbs and to pray for wisdom every day. He told me there are promises of wisdom and knowledge and understanding in these two life hacks. Although "life hack" was not used back in the nineties, the theory behind the slang was still the same. So, I read a Proverb every day and read the book of Proverbs every month, and I prayed. Oh, how I reminded God of His promise to pour out wisdom upon the one who asks of it, and I reminded Him that I was the one asking.

My desire for wisdom and knowledge grew deeper and stronger without the resources to attain it in a traditional way. I read my Bible through and through—Genesis to Revelation, Genesis to Malachi, Matthew to Revelation, sometimes yearly, sometimes monthly. Always daily. I gave myself goals of timeline accomplishments. I wrote a list of words that I did not know, and I looked them up in a dictionary to learn their purpose. I did this with secular books, too. I read and learned from the books that "smart people" read, Shakespeare and Dickens and Alex Haley.

Another day during my years at Bible college, I prayed for academic knowledge. I concluded that if God could give His wisdom and knowledge to any of us who ask, then why couldn't He give academic knowledge, too. So, I prayed, and I studied, and I failed, and I tried again, and I learned, and I graduated with a double major.

I started praying for specific areas of wisdom and knowledge as the years passed. After getting married, I prayed. When my husband asked me to "do the books," I prayed. Holding my newborn, I prayed. Speaking to women at my first Bible study, I prayed. In all my experiences, I prayed for wisdom *and* for knowledge.

Today, as I write this study on a book that I battle with so terribly, I pray. And in my prayer for wisdom and knowledge, I see, *"but we have the mind of Christ."*[9] I sit silently in this truth.

---

[9] 1 Corinthians 2:16

Scripture:

And I, when I came to you, brothers,
did not come proclaiming to you the testimony of God
with lofty speech or wisdom.
For I decided to know nothing among you
except Jesus Christ and him crucified.
And I was with you in weakness
and in fear and much trembling,
and my speech and my message
were not in plausible words of wisdom,
but in demonstration of the Spirit and of power,
so that your faith might not rest in the wisdom of men
but in the power of God.
1 Corinthians 2:1–5

Paul's society highly favored having knowledge of God. Raised as a devout Jew from the lineage of Benjamin,[10] he learned and excelled under the teaching of the Jewish teacher, Gameliel.[11] This deep knowledge in the Old Testament scriptures and Jewish laws rooted a zeal within Paul's soul. We know what he did with that zeal.[12] We know that he lived to accomplish much out of his knowledge of God. Then Jesus Christ introduced himself to Paul.[13]

This is when I began to relate to Paul and when my opinion of him began to shift. He had such a religious upbringing with a dominant stand in the Pharisaical sect. He learned all there was to learn; he put all that he had learned into action. His knowledge was his sword and his defense. It was in this knowledge that he judged all else. He searched out anyone who opposed the knowledge of the Old Testament law bringing these people before the courts and even standing in the presence of their death.[14] His knowledge of God blinded him from the truth of Jesus Christ.

---

[10] Romans 11:1; Philippians 3:5
[11] Acts 5:34, 22:3
[12] Introduction: About Paul; Book of Acts
[13] Acts 9:1–22
[14] Acts 7:54–8:1

This statement breaks my heart for him. His knowledge of God did not bring him into a relationship with God. If it did, he would have understood Jesus to be the prophesied Messiah; therefore, Jesus would have counted him among the twelve. I wonder if Paul ever wished for his story to be different. I wonder if he ever regretted his zeal. Then I wonder if he ever found true peace within himself during those dark moments within his thoughts remembering who he killed out of religious zeal.

Scripture:

> ...so that your faith might not rest in the wisdom
> of men but in the power of God.
> Yet among the mature we do impart wisdom,
> although it is not a wisdom of this age
> or of the rulers of this age, who are doomed to pass away.
> But we impart a secret and hidden wisdom of God,
> which God decreed before the ages for our glory.
> 1 Corinthians 2:5–7

Wisdom is an attainable thing, often a thing we all desire, and most definitely a thing learned. As humans, we attain measurable wisdom simply by living. Wisdom is the discerning or judging of a matter to see if it is right or true or a lasting idea. Life teaches us wisdom. Paul wants to place a sharp contrast between the wisdom that we attain in our humanity and the wisdom we receive from the Holy Spirit through Jesus Christ.

He also wants to place a sharp contrast between wisdom that we learn from men or religious teachings and wisdom from God. Separating one wisdom from the other is difficult, especially when our authority teaches us to live under the wisdom of man via religious teachings. For wisdom of man seeps into our very being, so that, when we hear of a contrasting concept, we battle guilt and uncertainty. In this, fear and insecurity overwhelm.

Paul models a brilliant suggestion in citing this contrast. Use a two-edged sword. Look again at what he said in verse two, "*For I decided to know nothing among you except Jesus Christ and him crucified."* Paul studied Jesus Christ. He knew God, but he met Jesus and craved to follow Him. This is the mighty power of the wisdom of God. His wisdom cuts to the heart of all wisdom. And Paul chose to neglect all his Biblical teaching as he studied Jesus Christ. This is brilliant. And slightly nerve-wracking. For knowledge brings confidence and drive. Paul had both. But he chose to start over. All confidence in his knowledge and wisdom was set aside. All drive to silence the name of Jesus diminished to a mere nothing.

Everything was new and frightfully uncomfortable. Mr. Status-quo was scared—shaking in his boots and stumbling over his words. This is not the same person we compare ourselves to or desire to hold a match next to. You know who he was? A follower of Jesus who was learning how to follow Jesus by studying Jesus through the gift of wisdom—wisdom that was in him since the moment he chose to follow Jesus.

This is you and me. This is our truth. We have knowledge and wisdom that have naturally settled their place in our heads. Then we met Jesus. We, too, have the wisdom of God in us. We, too, have the choice to make as to which form of wisdom we cling to, utilize, and grow.

Oh, that we follow Paul in his example and become students of Jesus Christ! If you are engaged in an internal religious battle, I pray you will set your battle aside. Perhaps write each of those war-zone statements on a piece of paper, then read the story of Jesus and His heart of love. You will find His words written within the first four books of the New Testament (Matthew–John). You will read of His heart, His actions, His manners, His responses, and His purpose. As you read these books, I genuinely believe you will find truths to write over the statements on your paper. Over time and through His truth, you will silence the war within. You will grow in wisdom of God. You will experience a whole new feeling of freedom to be the child of God you were destined to be. Not in man's wisdom but in God's.

Scripture:

> *None of the rulers of this age understood this,*
> *for if they had,*
> *they would not have crucified the Lord of glory.*

> *But, as it is written,*
> *"What no eye has seen, nor ear heard,*
> *nor the heart of man imagined,*
> *what God has prepared for those who love him"*[15]
> *these things God has revealed to us through the Spirit.*[16]
> *1 Corinthians 2:8–10a*

This wisdom of God is the very thing that shakes up our religious beliefs. I know not all religious beliefs are bad, but the ones that sit in opposition to the character of Jesus Christ are equally bad and harmful. The wisdom of God shakes up our rules and standards, allowing them to settle into a place of grace, love, and eternal purpose. It settles our comparisons and condemnations among the body of Christ. And it frees us of our own pride, offering grace and love and eternal purpose in its place. Yes, the wisdom of God is a solid foundation on which we build our personal connection to our Savior Jesus Christ.

The religious leaders of the day did not receive God's wisdom. They had an intense knowledge of God and of His law, but they lacked an understanding of Jesus and the Holy Spirit.

It is the Holy Spirit of God that Paul is introducing to the Corinthian believers in verse nine. Remember, believing in the resurrected Christ was a new belief at this time. Also, the filling of the Holy Spirit was a brand-new gift from God to those who believed in His Son. This was all new, only decades old.

---

[15] Isaiah 64:4
[16] John 14:26; Ephesians 3:3–12

The Holy Spirit was indeed a mystery, but a mystery given to us as a gift of understanding. The more we know about the Holy Spirit, the less He is a mystery.

From the beginning of time to the first verse in the written Scriptures to eternity, God the Father, God the Son, and God the Holy Spirit have existed as the One and only God. Scripture spills this out from cover to cover. Nature screams it out from every season to every cell to every star that shines in its night sky. God is God; He is the Creator, the lover of our souls, and the giver of life. This is the simplest and most complex truth to comprehend. This truth, my friend, is the beginning of the wisdom of God.

Scripture:

For the Spirit searches everything,
even the depths of God.
For who knows a person's thoughts
except the spirit of that person,
which is in him?
So also no one comprehends
the thoughts of God
except the Spirit of God.

Now we have received
not the spirit of the world,
but the Spirit who is from God,
that we might understand
the things freely given us by God.
And we impart this in words
not taught by human wisdom
but taught by the Spirit,
interpreting spiritual truths
to those who are spiritual.

The natural person does not accept
the things of the Spirit of God,
for they are folly to him,

and he is not able to understand them
because they are spiritually discerned.
The spiritual person judges all things,
but is himself to be judged by no one.

"For who has understood the mind of the Lord
so as to instruct him?"
But we have the mind of Christ.
1 Corinthians 2:10b–16

Do you remember Evian water? Sure, it is still around — as are Aqua Net, Aussie, and Vo5. These brands were advertised to be the answer to our problems. Of all the brands advertised when I was a kid, Evian was the one I longed for the most. To me it was an image that stated you had it all. To walk around with your head high and an expensive bottle of Evian water casually in your hand was the ultimate image I desired. It is comical how my heart is beaming in its reminiscence of a desired bottle of water. I don't know if I ever did get a sip of the water. By the time I could afford it, I chose a different brand to wrap my freshly painted fingernails around, Starbucks. Liquid brands matter to me. Immensely. I am giggling at this proclaimed realization. Even today when I set out on a trip, I grab a latte from The Human Bean and a tall, sleek Voss before starting my journey with my head high. Liquid brands. How funny.

It only makes sense that when I think of the Holy Spirit in the simplest logic that I picture a sealed bottle of water. No brand, form, shape, or size — just sealed. That is the Holy Spirit in you. A full bottle of water sealed shut — where a drop cannot add or spill from it — placed within us as a gift from God upon our relationship with Jesus Christ. The brand? You. The image? God — full and always. In every moment of every day, the sealed bottle of water will not spill out a single drop. That is the promise that comes with the gift of receiving the Holy Spirit.

Do you feel it? Upon receiving Jesus Christ as your Savior, the longing for the answer to life is gone. Do you feel that absence of wondering and feel that place of belonging? That is the Holy Spirit in you. Or when you are on your knees in prayer over something too big to manage on your own, a feeling seeps into your heart that settles you. You feel as if a silence holds your heart despite the chaos that rages. You say you cannot explain it — that there is a peace that passes your understanding. Ah! That is true, for that is the Holy Spirit in you.

Do you see it? That vice that has had its little trap set around you appears to have loosened its grip. This thing that has often been a struggle, a battle, is losing its importance. You may have attempted to fight it before, but then you would give in. Frustration in this cycle is ever present. Then you begin praying about it. You find yourself asking the Lord for His help in this battle with that vice, and you notice something is different. The satisfaction is not the same. And you begin to feel free, alive, and new. That is the Holy Spirit in you.

Not that there is more of Him in you. No. He sealed you, remember. Not a drop added to it. Not a drop can seep out. But in time, there becomes more of you in Him. More of His presence begins to shine out of you. More of His conviction and guidance begins to form you into the image of God.

Do you hear it? Conversations at work, responses to your spouse, reactions to your children, thoughts within, and so on. You hear yourself say things and wonder where *that* came from. You were nice, and you meant it. You forgave, and you felt it. You had patience, and you did not know that was even possible. The very tone of your voice begins to change, not because of your determination, but because the Holy Spirit is in you.

It is vital that we grasp the gift of the Holy Spirit. When it is about the Spirit, it is about you. He is a personal and individual gift to you. And He is a personal, individual gift to me. If we are each filled and sealed with the Holy Spirit, then imagine what He can do in and through us for the Glory of God and the furthering of the Name of Jesus Christ!

This is Paul's point. Listen again to his declaration of the presence and the purpose of the Holy Spirit.

Scripture:

> *For the Spirit searches everything,*
> *even the depths of God.*
> *For who knows a person's thoughts*
> *except the spirit of that person,*
> *which is in him?*
> *So also no one comprehends*
> *the thoughts of God*
> *except the Spirit of God.*
>
> *Now we have received*
> *not the spirit of the world,*
> *but the Spirit who is from God,*
> *that we might understand*
> *the things freely given us by God.*
> *And we impart this in words not*
> *taught by human wisdom*
> *but taught by the Spirit,*
> *interpreting spiritual truths*
> *to those who are spiritual.*
>
> *The natural person does not accept*
> *the things of the Spirit of God,*
> *for they are folly to him,*
> *and he is not able to understand them*
> *because they are spiritually discerned.*
> *The spiritual person judges all things,*
> *but is himself to be judged by no one.*
>
> *"For who has understood the mind of the Lord*
> *so as to instruct him?"*
> *But we have the mind of Christ.*
> *1 Corinthians 2:10b–16*

I may not drink Evian to quench my thirst after a workout, and I may only sip at a Voss periodically, but the Living Water that does not run dry is full within me. Not because of my brand but because of the image of

God in which He created me. I am His and He is mine. The Holy Spirit is a promised gift to me, and His presence is evident: Of this I am confident.

I am confident of this because the Holy Spirit is alive. He was not merely a gift given on the day of salvation. He is alive and present every moment of every day. To have the gift of the Spirit in your life is a personal gift from God. The Spirit identifies you as a child of God. It is personal to have the Holy Spirit in and with you. It is also universal within the body of Christ. Every believer has the Holy Spirit — sealed in His fullness.

The Holy Spirit becomes an unsettling conversation at times or a completely ignored entity simply because He is harder to define. It is easy to define God the Father, for He is the great I AM. He is the Creator and the sustainer of life. He is our Father and our hiding place. God the Son is defined by His name. Just the power in His name brings a shattering definition. Jesus Christ is the Savior of the world. He is our brother, our friend, the Rock on which we stand. He is the door, the bread, and the Word that was from the beginning. God the Holy Spirit is our comforter and our guide. And then we may linger. I did. I did not know the Spirit growing up. Preachers often presented Him in a smaller light. All to grow up and read for myself repeatedly that Jesus, as man, promised to send the Holy Spirit after He ascends to Heaven. Jesus promised the Holy Spirit's presence to His followers as comforter post His own departure.[17]

The Creator God did not design death and heartache. He created all things and called them good. He breathed life into the very dirt He created and called it good. He designed woman out of His created man and called her complete. God created life. Satan, however, brought forth sin, death, and the seed of evil now born within each of us. God did not design these, so Jesus came to defeat them. He put death where it belongs: In the pit of hell. Eternal life sits before us through Jesus' silencing of the grave. And as we remain in this good life and in our good, created selves, we have the Holy Spirit. Why? Because life and living in the midst of sin, death and evil are hard.

---

[17] John 14:16, 14:26, 15:26, 16:7

Jesus lived and purposed to relate fully and intentionally with us in this difficult reality. He learned obedience to His parents.[18] He felt tidal waves of emotions during heartbreaking situations.[19] He endured the pain of a back-stabbing friend.[20] He had the frustration of being misunderstood.[21] He embraced God's eternal plan knowing there's no turning back.[22] Jesus experienced it all without ever sinning.[23] Frequently, He remained in communion with God to refrain from the temptation of sin. Jesus contended with the flesh moment-by-moment for God's prized creation. Therefore, the Holy Spirit has come to make life not so hard. And to return the very act of living to what God designed it to be: good.

For too many years, I allowed my insufficiency in academia to hold me back. My insecurities became a crutch to my inabilities. Then one day, I spilled it all in a coffee shop Bible-study meeting. Standing there before a room full of women, I shared my educational history for the first time. I shared my deepest scar and loudest cry. The truth is, as I detailed my story, its depth began to weaken. I heard my words but no longer felt the wound.

A woman sat in the back row listening with the most intent expression in her eyes. Part of my mind wanted to keep going, to just share it with a heart who clearly needed to hear my story. The other part of my mind wanted to stop talking and ask her if she wanted to be my friend. God knew I was going to share my story that day. God also knew that she needed to hear it.

It did not take long for Rhiannon's status as Bible study attender to switch over to one of the most treasured jewels on my heart. God healed my story simply by sharing it with a listening soul. Together, she and I walk in the wisdom and knowledge of God despite our stories of academic expertise.

---

[18] Luke 2:48–49
[19] John 11:35; Matthew 21:12
[20] John 13:26–27; Matthew 26:69–75
[21] Mark 9:14–23
[22] John 2:1–11
[23] 2 Corinthians 5:21

All this to say, it is immaterial how you rate on the academic scale or in your knowledge of the wisdom of God. What matters is whether you know Jesus Christ as your Savior. If you do not, then allow me to introduce Him to you.[24] If you do, then hear the words of 1 Corinthians 2:16, *"But {you} have the mind of Christ."*

Does this make you want to sit silently with me? In your faith in God the Father, He gives you the Spirit of God and the mind of His Son. In Him, you are the fullness of all wisdom and knowledge and understanding. It is already in you. It is now up to you to utilize it, grow it, and use it for the glory of God.

---

[24] Introduction: Jesus Christ

Jaclyn Palmer

Notes

1 Corinthians 3

But I, brothers, could not address you as spiritual people, but as people of the
flesh, as infants in Christ. I fed you with milk, not solid food, for you were not
ready for it. And even now you are not yet ready, for you are still of the flesh.
For while there is jealousy and strife among you, are you not of the flesh
and behaving only in a human way? For when one says, "I follow Paul,"
and another, "I follow Apollos," are you not being merely human?

What then is Apollos? What is Paul? Servants through whom you believed,
as the Lord assigned to each. I planted, Apollos watered, but God gave
the growth. So neither he who plants nor he who waters is anything,
but only God who gives the growth. He who plants and he who waters
are one, and each will receive his wages according to his labor.
For we are God's fellow workers. You are God's field, God's building.

According to the grace of God given to me, like a skilled master builder I laid a
foundation, and someone else is building upon it. Let each one take care how he
builds upon it. For no one can lay a foundation other than that which is laid,
which is Jesus Christ. Now if anyone builds on the foundation with gold, silver,
precious stones, wood, hay, straw — each one's work will become manifest, for
the Day will disclose it, because it will be revealed by fire, and the fire will test
what sort of work each one has done. If the work that anyone has built on the
foundation survives, he will receive a reward. If anyone's work is burned up, he
will suffer loss, though he himself will be saved, but only as through fire.

Do you not know that you are God's temple and that God's Spirit
dwells in you? If anyone destroys God's temple, God will destroy him.
For God's temple is holy, and you are that temple.

Let no one deceive himself. If anyone among you thinks that he is wise in this age, let him become a fool that he may become wise. For the wisdom of this world is folly with God. For it is written, "He catches the wise in their craftiness," and again, "The Lord knows the thoughts of the wise, that they are futile." So let no one boast in men. For all things are yours, whether Paul or Apollos or Cephas or the world or life or death or the present or the future — all are yours, and you are Christ's, and Christ is God's.

3

You Are His Temple

For we are God's fellow workers.
You are ... God's building.
According to the grace of God given to me,
like a skilled master builder I laid a foundation,
and someone else is building upon it.
Let each one take care how he builds upon it.
Do you not know that you are God's temple
and that God's Spirit dwells in you?
1 Corinthians 3:9–10, 16

God knows the heart of gold for one is an act of wood for another. Barnabas is a great example of this truth. He was a man who owned land: an average person in an ordinary situation. Church tradition says that landowners often used their land as a burial plot, but the details of the land are unknown—quantity, location, history, value, etcetera. All we really know about this land is its owner, Barnabas.

We meet Barnabas as we read Acts 4. We learn his birth name was Joseph, but the apostles gave him the name Barnabas because of the abundant encouragement he bestowed upon them. He was born into the lineage of Levi, the priestly line of the nation of Israel. Scripture tells us that he was a follower of Jesus, an encourager to the apostles, a Levite from Cypress, and a landowner.

Lastly, we see he has a giving heart that a couple attempts to emulate.

There was a couple who owned land: an average couple in an ordinary situation. Although we know their names to be Ananias and Sapphira, we know nothing about their land. No knowledge of its size, location, history, or quality. All we know about the land are its owners, Ananias and Sapphira.

We know a little bit about these owners. We know their names and their marital status. They trusted each other in their shared financial commitments. We quickly learn how they were both willing to lie with eyes diverted from the face of the King of kings. Ananias and Sapphira were followers of Jesus and landowners. This couple saw what Barnabas had done; they did the same thing.

One act. Two hearts: One with a heart of gold, the other of wood.

Scripture:

> *Thus Joseph, who was also called by the apostles Barnabas*
> *(which means son of encouragement), a Levite, a native of Cyprus,*
> *sold a field that belonged to him and brought the money*
> *and laid it at the apostles' feet.*
> *But a man named Ananias, with his wife Sapphira,*
> *sold a piece of property, and with his wife's knowledge*
> *he kept back for himself some of the proceeds and brought*
> *only a part of it and laid it at the apostles' feet.*
> *Acts 4:36–5:2*

In context with this chapter, you and I are God's fellow workers. We are God's building (v. 9). This means we are equally the builders and the building. Did you have a mental image of being Bob the Builder hitting yourself with his trusty little hammer? Yeah, okay, neither did I. Either way, this is our reality. We are the ones doing the work, and we are the ones on which we are working. I say that we gather our little golden hammers and get to work.

We each need our own hammers because spiritual building is about each of us. It is about knowing our foundation. The foundation is Jesus Christ. Period. There is no other foundation for a Christian to build upon.[25] Our foundation is sure,[26] it is trustworthy,[27] and it is eternal.[28] I do not think there is a follower of Jesus out there that debates the validity of our foundation. Looking back at Chapter 1, even the divided Corinthians stood unified in the declaration of the name of Jesus Christ. Our foundation is not the issue.

The issue is the building of the temple. God places us on the sure foundation, then we work on the same temple that has been under construction since the Corinthian believers. What a powerful thought to know we are working on the same structure as this infant body two thousand years ago!

Like anything new, these believers had to learn how to do everything. Grasping truths about Jesus Christ being the way, the truth, and the life was easy. That fire spread. But the other infant functions of hand-eye coordination, walking independently, and transitioning from milk to meat (1 Corinthians. 3:1–2) were challenging for these new believers. And it should have been. New is hard.

And here we stand on the foundation of Christ with a free mind to choose how we are going to build. We see the six resources listed: gold, silver, precious stones, wood, hay, straw. And this entire process sounds so new, so hard. But like the early Corinthian believers, we, too, need to get to work.

---

[25] Matthew 7:24–27; Acts 4:12
[26] Hebrews 6:19
[27] 1 Timothy 1:15; Revelation 21:5
[28] John 3:16, 10:28, 17:3

Jaclyn Palmer

Scripture:

For no one can lay a foundation
other than that which is laid,
which is Jesus Christ.
Now if anyone builds on the foundation
with gold, silver, precious stones, wood, hay, straw —
1 Corinthians 3:11–12

When I read 1 Corinthians 3, I think of the difference that pours out of us as we perform the same deeds. Even deeper still, I think of the difference that pours out of me as I perform the same deeds. Take, for example, me being a door holder at church. I smile as I type this pronouncement. I smile because this position used to be humiliating to me. I smile because I have learned to love it wholeheartedly.

Years ago, I reluctantly became a door holder on Sunday mornings. Me, the Sunday School teacher, the sister of the pastor's wife, Jaclyn the great. I had zero desire to stand at a door and say hello to people. Zero. But I did it. Friend, I pretended that my heart was gold, but that was all an act of wood. I built upon the foundation of Jesus Christ with nothing but splintered wood.

Fast forward fifteen years, and I volunteered to serve in the First Impressions Team at my church. To volunteer for such a ministry means holding the door open and saying hello to people I do not know. Friend, I love this ministry! I love when the elderly appreciates an easy entrance into the house of God. I love when a woman stands taller as I compliment her hair or purse or shoes or all these things. I love it when I watch her husband beam with agreement at his smiling bride. I love when littles walk eagerly into God's house knowing their Sunday School class is waiting for their giggles to join in. I love this ministry. Sometimes, I feel like what I do is wood, but God sees my heart of gold. I am building upon the foundation with glittering gold.

One act. Two hearts. God knows the heart of our work.

In our work, we are personally responsible for how we build and which resources we choose to use. The catchy part is, God knows our hearts. He knows when we serve with a heart of gold. He knows when our pretentious heart of silver is an act of flammable hay. He knows when we feel like all we have to offer is straw, yet He beholds our heart as a precious stone. Friend, be honest with yourself. God knows your heart.

- I am personally responsible for the materials I use to build me.
- You are personally responsible for the materials you use to build you.

You and I personally create the church of God. You and I are the Church, individually and corporately. Do you see the big picture? Do you see your impact? Do you see the power that you have to construct the church of God with the right materials?

Gold. Silver. Precious stones. In the Old Testament, men used these three materials to construct the physical temple of God. Scripture beautifully details the use of these materials in Solomon's construction of the temple.[29] Throughout its descriptive construction, gold, silver, and precious stones embellish the building process of the temple. Oh, to see how richly it glittered the evidence of being God's house![30]

Wood. Hay. Straw. These three materials get a bad rap because they are flammable. I get that concept but allow me to state this one simple truth. God created these three items by His hand; they cradled His infancy and supported His final breath. We do not magnify these items, but we do not deny their availability and usefulness to display the brightness of His personal work of love. They were natural elements that got the job done. No, they do not have an eternal gain, nor do they offer any substantial growth. But at times they can be useful and efficient.

Gold, silver, precious stones. What are they to you? How can you dig for gold, search for silver, and display precious stones in you today? Take

---

[29] 2 Chronicles 2
[30] Ezra 4:4

Paul's warning of how to build the heart and shine the evidence of being His. Oh, to see how richly you shine the evidence of being God's house!

Scripture:

*Do you not know that you are God's temple
and that God's Spirit dwells in you?*
1 Corinthians 3:16

This is where the beauty of this passage begins to shine. This is where we see ourselves for who we are. Collectively, we are the temple of God. Individually, you are the temple of God. Truly, you are His dwelling place. Does this truth overwhelm your heart? Does it allow you to feel important and valued and dignified and loved and full? Does it make you stand[31] a little taller, speak[32] a little bolder, work[33] a little stronger? You. Are. His. Church. If anything from this study hits you like a feathered ton of bricks, I pray it is this truth. You are His temple, and you matter to God.

Now that we know that we are the temple of God, we need to learn how to build our "product" so we can accomplish the "production" needed. I pray we do not lose focus on this point. I am not defending selfishness. I am proclaiming your need to see yourself as God the Father sees you. All too often our vision of who we are becomes dimmed by the elements of our surroundings.

Do you know you are the temple of God? You are His church. You must take care of it. You must tend to it. Feed it. Exercise it. Move it. Pamper it. Love it. Embrace it. Speak kindly to it. Nurture it. Grow it. Water it. Know what the temple of God is! The temple of God is *you.*

As the daughter of God, you are the gold needed to construct this most beautiful structure. Saved through the blood of Jesus Christ, you have the

---

[31] Ephesians 4:11–14
[32] Ephesians 6:19; Acts 9:27
[33] 1 Corinthians 16:13

silver required to shine His Light in and through this building. Filled with the Holy Spirit, you pour out the precious stones that magnify the very beauty of the Lord. Oh, Friend, you are beautiful. God sees and values you as you are. He created you to represent the image of God. That is who you are. You are His.

With a proper vision and a pure heart, we can confidently grab our little hammers and get to work. If there is something inside you that is prohibiting your ability to focus on your personal work on yourself, then look at Paul's substantial warning. His caution to us makes the building process incredibly personal.

Scripture:

> *If anyone destroys God's temple,*
> *God will destroy him.*
> *For God's temple is holy,*
> *And you are that temple.*
> 1 Corinthians 3:17

Do you see how personal this is? He has righteous anger toward anyone who destroys His Church. Any good mom can understand this righteous anger. Has your child come home from school with a black eye? Have you ever spotted your child sitting alone with tears in her eyes? Have you ever consoled your child's broken heart? It does not matter how old our child is. If someone hurts our child, that person will no longer be alive. Well, according to our feelings anyway. We are not *actually* going to kill anyone.

That feeling we as moms can resonate with is a small understanding of how God feels when someone defiles His child. If God hates when His child is defiled by another, then why do we hurt, defile, or destroy ourselves?

The negative thoughts we have about ourselves, the hurtful words or deeds we allow others to say or do to us, the innocent temptations we allow to overtake us are all enemies to us in the eyes of our precious

Creator. God hates that. It breaks His heart. We would never stand by allowing anyone to treat our child the way we treat ourselves. God says, *do not defile my temple for the temple is holy. You are my temple.* It is vital that we take our position as the temple of God with utmost care, for what we do with our individual temples will affect one another's individual temples.

Remember your foundation is Jesus Christ. God created you, saved you through Jesus Christ, and filled you with the Holy Spirit. Remember that your very creation was perfectly designed by the hands of God the Father. Know how thoroughly loved you are by Jesus Christ. And recognize that the Holy Spirit's power to become your full design is freely given to you. Do you know that you are the temple of God!

There was a body of believers. An average body in an ordinary situation. This body was among the first of the early church. We can list a name or two, but we do not know much about their pasts, their stories, their struggles, their successes, or their failures. All we really know about this body of believers is their foundation: Jesus.

We do know a little more about the body of believers than we know about individuals. This body was present at Pentecost—numbered with the three thousand. These were the first (post the apostles) to receive the power of the Holy Spirit and faithfully devote themselves to Jesus' teaching, remembering Jesus through the breaking of bread and in prayer. Together, this church had all things in common: followers of Jesus, filled with the Holy Spirit, and unified one with the other.

The heart of this immense body of Christ was unheard of. Acts 4:32–35 continues the description of these 3,000—plus those added daily. There was a fire spread through the city of Jerusalem. Old Testament believers clung fully to the fulfilled prophecy they had been waiting for. These individuals were the first to stand on the foundation of Jesus Christ, the risen Savior. They were the first filled with the fire of the Holy Spirit of God, truly faithful workers who set a solid blueprint of what a structured building looks like.

When we read all 47 verses of Acts Chapter 2, we see the full background of Barnabas, Ananias, and Sapphira. These three average individuals were part of this extraordinary body of believers.

Scripture:

Now the full number of those who believed were of one heart and soul,
and no one said that any of the things that belonged to him was his own,
but they had everything in common.
And with great power the apostles were giving their testimony
to the resurrection of the Lord Jesus,
and great grace was upon them all.
There was not a needy person among them,
for as many as were owners of lands or houses sold them and brought
the proceeds of what was sold and laid it at the apostles' feet,
and it was distributed to each as any had need.
Acts 4:32–35

One unified heart of gold for God. One united act of selling their lands and laying the proceeds at the apostles' feet. Each gift given for the glory of God. They were fully united. Except for two, Ananias and Sapphira. As Acts Chapter 4 concludes with Barnabas' sacrificial gift, Acts Chapter 5 begins with this couple's lie. They did the common work of gold with a flammable deception in their heart. Scripture eerily details the falsehood rehearsed by both husband and wife and the repercussion of their deception.[34]

Nowhere else in Scripture do we read about Ananias and Sapphira. Their lives and their historical stories end the moment they fatally expressed the intentional evil scripted in their hearts. On the other hand, we see Barnabas throughout the New Testament.[35] How I would love to detail his story, but his heart easily lends itself to another book of its own. I must, however, whisper the teeny bits of his story. Because, if you are like me, you are highly curious about this sweet follower of Jesus.

---

[34] Acts 5:1–11
[35] Acts 4:36–37, 9:27, 11:24, 13:1–15:39; 1 Corinthians 9:6; Galatians 2:1–13; Colossians 4:10

Five chapters after meeting Barnabas in Acts 4, we see him as the voice that defended Saul's conversion. He stood up for Saul and settled the apostles' fear as Saul stood before them. Barnabas discipled Saul. He taught Saul how to be a follower of Jesus. He did not know that he was training the "Great Apostle Paul"; he was merely teaching Jesus' message to a new convert named Saul.

On the first missionary journey, Saul takes on the name "Paul" to be more effective in his ministry.[36] Paul becomes the leading authority in their ministry together. Barnabas remained faithful to his character of encouragement throughout this transition. For Barnabas knew it was not about how they did their work but about Who they were doing it for. We will see Barnabas again in 1 Corinthians 9 where Paul references him as a faithful man of character. Barnabas was simply a follower of Jesus who built upon the foundation with love, truth, and faithfulness.

Scripture:

Let no one deceive himself.
If anyone among you thinks that he is wise in this age,
let him become a fool that he may become wise.
For the wisdom of this world is folly with God.
For it is written,
"He catches the wise in their craftiness,"
and again, "The Lord knows
the thoughts of the wise, that they are futile."
So let no one boast in men.

For all things are yours,
whether Paul or Apollos or Cephas or the world
or life or death or the present or the future —
all are yours,
and you are Christ's,
and Christ is God's.
1 Corinthians 3:18–23

---

[36] Acts 13

As New Testament followers of Jesus, we ought to learn from Ananias and Sapphira. When we rely on our own wisdom, it can easily turn into internal deception, sometimes without our realizing it. We analyze situations and justify deeds to the point of shifted eyes. Once our eyes shift from the face of God, we are then deceived by ourselves.

This truth does not fill us with a dread of hopelessness. Rather, this truth is a gift of freedom from our God. You see, He knows our wisdom and our weakness and our flesh. So, God offered us a solution, a foundation to stand upon, and tools to build ourselves up with.

Do not ruin your temple with comparison. Let us lift our pastors and leaders in prayer not in position. May we see the world we live in as a gift from God not as a platform to attain. May we value our life as a gift from God. May we love it and live it. May we no longer see death as a heartache, but as Jesus' ultimate gift. For in His death, He exchanged its curse of eternal separation from God to eternal life with Him.

Gold. Silver. Precious stones. Each tool builds and grows and glistens as we seek more wisdom, attain more knowledge, and practice more understanding. Little by little, we drop those stones of judgment that we cast upon ourselves. We see ourselves in the light of who we are, for we are the temple of God. All that is going on around us and all that is going to happen is a gift to us. No longer do we face life on a shaken foundation. We have a place to stand, a place to proclaim.

You are a precious gift given to Jesus Christ by God, a gift for Jesus to have and to hold,[37] a gift He promises to never let go.[38] You are held. You are loved. You are His.

---

[37] John 10:27–30
[38] Hebrews 13:5

51

Jaclyn Palmer

Notes

1 Corinthians 4

This is how one should regard us, as servants of Christ and stewards of the mysteries of God. Moreover, it is required of stewards that they be found faithful. But with me it is a very small thing that I should be judged by you or by any human court. In fact, I do not even judge myself. For I am not aware of anything against myself, but I am not thereby acquitted. It is the Lord who judges me. Therefore do not pronounce judgment before the time, before the Lord comes, who will bring to light the things now hidden in darkness and will disclose the purposes of the heart. Then each one will receive his commendation from God.

I have applied all these things to myself and Apollos for your benefit, brothers, that you may learn by us not to go beyond what is written, that none of you may be puffed up in favor of one against another. For who sees anything different in you? What do you have that you did not receive? If then you received it, why do you boast as if you did not receive it?

Already you have all you want! Already you have become rich! Without us you have become kings! And would that you did reign, so that we might share the rule with you! For I think that God has exhibited us apostles as last of all, like men sentenced to death, because we have become a spectacle to the world, to angels, and to men. We are fools for Christ's sake, but you are wise in Christ. We are weak, but you are strong. You are held in honor, but we in disrepute. To the present hour we hunger and thirst, we are poorly dressed and buffeted and homeless, and we labor, working with our own hands. When reviled, we bless; when persecuted, we endure; when slandered, we entreat. We have become, and are still, like the scum of the world, the refuse of all things.

Jaclyn Palmer

I do not write these things to make you ashamed, but to admonish you as my beloved children. For though you have countless guides in Christ, you do not have many fathers. For I became your father in Christ Jesus through the gospel. I urge you, then, be imitators of me. That is why I sent you Timothy, my beloved and faithful child in the Lord, to remind you of my ways in Christ, as I teach them everywhere in every church. Some are arrogant, as though I were not coming to you. But I will come to you soon, if the Lord wills, and I will find out not the talk of these arrogant people but their power. For the kingdom of God does not consist in talk but in power. What do you wish? Shall I come to you with a rod, or with love in a spirit of gentleness?

4

The Heart of Judgment

This is how one should regard us,
as servants of Christ
and stewards of the mysteries of God.
Moreover, it is required of stewards
that they be found faithful.
1 Corinthians 4:1–2

The words of this book offer freedom from judging others' works with our own. If we remember who we are, and our hands are busy building upon that firm Foundation, then there is no finger space to hold or throw those condemning stones of judgment. Yet, we do. Paul declares, I am not the Judge, for "I do not even judge myself...It is the Lord who judges me." How free to claim this truth as a woman in society today. No longer would we condemn our appearances or actions, our decisions as a wife or as a mom, or how we worship or what we wear to church. We are free from self-judgment. Therefore, we are free to no longer compare ourselves to one another. God is our Judge, and our Judge loves each of us where we are.

Paul, as an apostle, is defending his case before his friends. What a sad reality. How heartbreaking to hear and to know that people you love are believing words spoken against you. Do you know this heartache? Do you feel the wound of that pain in your heart, in your soul, and repeating itself in your thoughts? This is Paul's anguish with his church body in Corinth. Imagine that internal fight.

Paul has a story. His past consists of religion, obedience, stature, and behaviors that glorified the law but broke the hearts of New Testament followers of Jesus Christ. He knows his story. They know his past. Satan knows, too.

I wonder how frequently he battled with the mental presence of his story. Did he struggle with Satan brutally reminding him of the scars of his past? I wonder if Christians throughout his journeys approached him with fear, with doubt of his true repentance, or of judgment of what he had done to someone they knew and loved.

Paul had to conquer the reputation of his past. He had to renew his mind into seeing himself in the newness of Christ Jesus. Paul had to determine to press forward to the prize of the high calling of God, rather than sit in the mire of what he once was.

Today, he must defend his reputation yet again.

This time, not considering his past, Paul declares his position as an apostle of Jesus Christ to people he loved. This is crazy. However, we can relate to this. May we heed Paul's words and follow him in his choice of self-evaluation in place of judgment.

Scripture:

> *But with me it is a very small thing*
> *that I should be judged by you*
> *or by any human court.*
> *In fact, I do not even judge myself.*
> *For I am not aware of anything against myself,*
> *but I am not thereby acquitted.*

It is the Lord who judges me.
1 Corinthians 4:3–4

To combat the verbal judgment thrown upon Paul, he sits down with Sosthenes,[39] a former religious Pharisee like himself and pens this very chapter we are holding in our hands today. Paul handed this letter to Timothy asking him to deliver it to the congregation of Corinth. Timothy, being young both in the Lord and in age, bravely complied with Paul's request. Beautiful to note that Paul would be admonishing Timothy years later to *"Let no one despise (judge) you for your youth."* [40] Rather, Timothy was to use his area of foreseen judgment as an opportunity to set an example of speech, of behavior, of love, of faith, and of purity.

How powerful to look upon our person and position and strength and weakness and past and story and future and our life as an opportunity to promote the love of Jesus Christ in us for the benefit of spiritual growth in others. How beautifully humbling it is to be a child of the King!

How precious is the depth of that reality! When Paul's loved ones cast judgment toward him, he shrugs. When the world around him demonstrates an opinion about him, he shrugs. When a thought crosses his mind about himself, he shrugs. He declares, I do not judge myself. God is the One, the only One, who judges me. God is aware of me, Paul says, and that is the only judgment that matters. Paul understood that he is merely a man, and God is eternally God. Oh, that we will see ourselves as Paul saw himself, as a child of God. That we will see one another as God sees each of us: His.

With God as our judge, we are free to build as discussed in the previous chapter. We are then free to self-evaluate as seems beneficial to our individual existence. Judgment stems from comparison, and that is not fair on any scale. It is not fair when comparison casts judgment on you from others or from you upon others. And it certainly is not fair when we compare ourselves among ourselves and find ourselves casting

[39] Introduction: Sosthenes
[40] 1 Timothy 4:12

internal judgment upon ourselves. Friend, God created you. God loves you. God is calling you to step closer and closer to Him moment by moment. Do not leave room in your mind for judgment. Judgment is a choice we must make, a behavior we must leave behind, a habit that must stop.

Christ Jesus offered us freedom from all forms of judgment the moment He rose from the dead. Walk in the gift of eternal life today! God has overwhelmed you with life. Embrace it. You are here to magnify His name as none other but *you*. Choose to shine His image brighter than the judgment that craves to diminish His light.

We may feel broken, empty and torn down. People in our lives desire to verbalize their opinion over us. But it is not their opinion that matters. Do not strive for their acceptance. Accept, rather, God's truth. Evaluate His truth in you. Examine, if you will, you and God. Examination is proper and sweet, personal, and private. It is you before your Creator with a pure heart and open ears to hear His truth spoken over you. Take in His words. Breathe in His love. Oh, that we will delight in examining ourselves in the truth of God's judgment of praise and love over us!

Scripture:

Therefore do not pronounce judgment
before the time, before the Lord comes,
who will bring to light
the things now hidden in darkness
and will disclose the purposes of the heart.
Then each one will receive his commendation from God.
1 Corinthians 4:5

Again, to examine is self; to judge is God. To accept is a reaction to living a life in the freedom of judgment. It is at this point that we sit at the feet of Jesus, protected in His judgment and His judgment alone. We begin to wonder, "But what about the world around me? What about the Christian that is defiling the name of Jesus? What about the preacher, the leader, the family member, the friend…?"

This thought—natural, healthy and good—is exactly the question they asked of Paul. He answers it in the next couple of chapters. Remember, we are in this study to find freedom *in* judgment not *from* judgment. Judgment is going to happen; we need to learn how to process it. Judgment must happen; we need to learn how to use it.

This may sound counterproductive to all we have studied these first four chapters. My prayer is that as we sit before Christ in our newfound mindset of how He sees us, we will find freedom and understanding as we look at those around us. Fair enough?

Scripture:

> *I have applied all these things to myself*
> *and Apollos for your benefit, brothers,*
> *that you may learn by us*
> *not to go beyond what is written,*
> *that none of you may be puffed up*
> *in favor of one against another.*
> *For who sees anything different in you?*
> *What do you have that you did not receive?*
> *If then you received it,*
> *why do you boast*
> *as if you did not receive it?*
> *1 Corinthians 4:6–7*

It is at this point that we find ourselves remembering 1 Corinthians Chapter 1. Here Paul addresses the details of the division that caused such an undertow of dissatisfaction, pride, and judgment within the Corinthian body of believers. Although some may easily hear truth and shift their eyes back to Jesus, others refrain from childlike faith. Some remain in their pride and position of stone throwing. We see this in the area of judgment toward apostles and preachers.

Apostles were men seen by Jesus—called and charged to proclaim the gospel message of Jesus Christ. Preachers or ministers are those who received that message, called by the Spirit of God to boldly proclaim the apostles' message of Jesus Christ—that is, the death, burial and resurrection of our Savior, Jesus Christ.

These men were human. Not elevated to lordship. Not compared to one another. Not treated as a king. They were men, namely servants, to the King who sits upon the Throne on the right side of God Almighty.

Within the body of Christ, small-group leaders were elevating themselves above the participants. They were allowing others to view them as something more than they were, servants of the body. Other leaders were comparing themselves to the position of apostleship, and in turn, elevating an apostle as something higher than designed to be, servant to the Servant of all.

In all this comparison, judgment was spilling out of human hearts blinded by pride. Behaviors granted Satan space within this first-century church. To silence Satan, Paul speaks boldly against pride and beckons them to see the truth of Christ-like servitude.

Scripture:

> *Already you have all you want!*
> *Already you have become rich!*
> *Without us you have become kings!*
> *And would that you did reign,*
> *so that we might share the rule with you!*
> *For I think that God has exhibited us apostles*
> *as last of all, like men sentenced to death,*
> *because we have become a spectacle*
> *to the world, to angels, and to men.*
> *We are fools for Christ's sake,*
> *but you are wise in Christ.*
> *We are weak, but you are strong.*
> *You are held in honor, but we in disrepute.*
> *To the present hour we hunger and thirst,*
> *we are poorly dressed and buffeted and homeless,*
> *and we labor, working with our own hands.*

> *When reviled, we bless;*
> *when persecuted, we endure;*
> *when slandered, we entreat.*
> *We have become, and are still,*
> *like the scum of the world,*
> *the refuse of all things.*
> *1 Corinthians 4:8–13*

Can you feel Paul's deep frustration with the haughty behavior spilling out of those called to be stewards of the gospel? Pride is gross. Self-elevation has no place in the Kingdom of God. Human elevation has no place, either. God alone lifted high! His Name magnified! Not Paul's, not a preacher's, not a leader's, not a man's, not a woman's — God. For this is the body of His Son, Jesus Christ. He alone sits on the Throne.

At this point, Paul writes one of his most noted lines. Consider the timing of his plea, the context of his urgency, and the audience to whom he speaks.

Paul is speaking directly to these leaders with words that do not support their opinion of themselves. Imagine the varying emotions that ran their course. He laid out an expressive liturgy of pride. Paul displays the leaders before the church as kings of wealth, power, and prestige. These three, Satan offered to Jesus.[41] I wonder if that truth coursed its way through any of their hearts. He follows this regal array with the reality of the apostles' everyday lifestyle. The apostles' call required faithful servanthood toward Jesus. Period.

The contrast between the air of those judging Paul via comparison and Paul's actual existence is astounding. You can hear the forethought of Paul's letter to the Philippian church where he will declare, *"Have this mind among yourselves…(Jesus) was in the form of God, did not count equality with God a thing to be grasped, but emptied himself, by taking the form of a servant…becoming obedient to the point of death…"*[42]

---

[41] Matthew 4:1–10
[42] Philippians 2:5–8

In this, Paul says, *"...be imitators of me..."*[43]

Scripture:

> *I do not write these things to make you ashamed,*
> *but to admonish you as my beloved children.*
> *For though you have countless guides in Christ,*
> *you do not have many fathers.*
> *For I became your father*
> *in Christ Jesus through the gospel.*
> *I urge you, then,*
> *be imitators of me.*
> *1 Corinthians 4:14–16*

There is a practical life lesson in the conclusion to this chapter: teach and be teachable. Jesus humbled himself to this when He came as a babe. He relinquished His knowledge of all things and allowed Mary to teach Him humanity. He walked among His creation in order to relate with them on all levels, except the level of human nature, which is sin. For it was sin itself that Jesus came to rid the world of. Yet, in His teachable spirit, Jesus taught His disciples and His followers the way, the truth, and the life. Jesus was equally teachable and able to teach.

Paul exhibited this same trait. In all his Biblical and Pharisaical knowledge, he forsook his level of knowledge and allowed first-century Christians to teach him the way and the truth and the life of Christ Jesus, his newfound Lord. Paul remained a student of the King yet taught the message of the gospel from city to city, heart to heart. Paul was equally teachable and able to teach.

The Corinthian leaders were struggling in both regards. They were truly battling for the ability to learn this position called "minister." They received this opportunity with pride rather than humility. They were fulfilling its call with their human limitations rather than through the leading of the Holy Spirit. The trait of being teachable was far from them in this season of learning.

---

[43] 1 Corinthians 11:1

These leaders were not teaching the purity of the gospel of Christ to the congregation. This is evident in the following two chapters. In their air of piety, they were allowing grotesque sin to permeate the reputation of Jesus followers. Paul called out the Corinthian leadership. Their words and their actions were in different volumes—both needed correcting.

Their need for correction brings us back to our earlier thought as we sat in the comfort of God's judgment over us: "But what about those around us?" In the following chapters we are going to see judgment as a tool, and we will learn how to use it and when to use it. I pray we will be teachable in this area. Not teachable to my words, or to Paul's for that matter, but to the heart and love of our Savior. I pray, also, that we will grasp these truths in such a way that we are able, in turn, to teach them to those under us.

Perhaps in your journey, the idea of teaching someone scriptural truth is too much too soon. Will you stand with Timothy and find your courage in Paul's admonition to use your spiritual youth as a sweet opportunity to demonstrate Christ in you? Claim 1 Timothy 4:12 as your life verse. Emulate Christ in you in all ways. Allow Christ to use your devotion to Him as a shining beacon of His love for humanity. You can do that. What a beautiful, teachable heart awaits in you!

Perhaps you have been teaching spiritual truth for quite some time, but this confusion of proper judgment has never been clear to you. With a teachable heart, will you walk with me in this study? Pray for wisdom, clarity, and understanding. Seek practicality in your life, your home, your ministry, and in your heart. Then go forth as a teacher of truth while you continue being a student of His Word.

Notes

1 Corinthians 5

It is actually reported that there is sexual immorality among you, and of a kind that is not tolerated even among pagans, for a man has his father's wife. And you are arrogant! Ought you not rather to mourn? Let him who has done this be removed from among you.

For though absent in body, I am present in spirit; and as if present, I have already pronounced judgment on the one who did such a thing. When you are assembled in the name of the Lord Jesus and my spirit is present, with the power of our Lord Jesus, you are to deliver this man to Satan for the destruction of the flesh, so that his spirit may be saved in the day of the Lord.

Your boasting is not good. Do you not know that a little leaven leavens the whole lump? Cleanse out the old leaven that you may be a new lump, as you really are unleavened. For Christ, our Passover lamb, has been sacrificed. Let us therefore celebrate the festival, not with the old leaven, the leaven of malice and evil, but with the unleavened bread of sincerity and truth.

I wrote to you in my letter not to associate with sexually immoral people — not at all meaning the sexually immoral of this world, or the greedy and swindlers, or idolaters, since then you would need to go out of the world. But now I am writing to you not to associate with anyone who bears the name of brother if he is guilty of sexual immorality or greed, or is an idolater, reviler, drunkard, or swindler — not even to eat with such a one. For what have I to do with judging outsiders? Is it not those inside the church whom you are to judge? God judges those outside. "Purge the evil person from among you."

5

The Time of Judgment

*It is actually reported
that there is sexual immorality among you,
and of a kind that is not tolerated
even among pagans,
for a man has his father's wife.
And you are arrogant!
Ought you not rather to mourn?
1 Corinthians 5:1–2a*

There are times as a teacher I do not want to teach. Recently, a woman asked me to teach on the topic of slavery. Freedom from slavery, specifically. No direction offered with this request. No story behind the heart that requested it. No Scripture desired for representation. No desired outcome. Simply, freedom from slavery. Interesting, I thought as I filed it away and pressed on teaching the topics of freedom that preceded this topic of slavery.

As time drew near, I found myself on my knees seeking the Lord for clear direction for this upcoming week's discussion. To be clearer, I asked God if I could dwell on Galatians 5. I told Him that discussing freedom from the chains of legalism would be freeing, dynamic, wonderful, and easy. My unsettled heart knew this was not what He was pressing. Romans 8 circled my mind each time I sought the Lord in prayer. Teaching on Romans 8 would center on teaching freedom from the chains of sin. There I sat with the Lord prepping my heart to teach a group of women how to name their sin and live in His freedom from slavery. I did not want to teach. You see, to teach on sin meant I must be honest about my own.

I have found freedom from the legalistic weight of constant sin and guilt. Yet, there is still the reality of being human. At times, in our humanity, we allow a comfortable existence of varying sins to bind us in chains. Again, I had to get real. I had to be authentic and vulnerable before these women. To equally relate to the chain of sin and the freedom from sin was necessary so that God could fully disclose the truth of this ever-important topic of freedom. This was one of those times in which I did not want to teach. Not one bit.

For a week, I scripturally and prayerfully prepared for this study, all the while asking God if we could switch course and flee to the comfortable topic of Galatians 5. There I sat before a crowded room of Bible students. All eyes on me. Stoic faces guarding their personal battles within. The whisper of the word sin hung heavily in the air. Freedom from sin sitting as an unwrapped present on our laps. Our choice lingered between longing for that beautiful gift with an unwillingness to exchange our sin for that gift.

Is there a harder topic to openly discuss than sin? The unteachable leaders from 1 Corinthians Chapter 4 did not battle with this. In fact, they welcomed sin into their church. Openly. Unabashedly. Not a stoic expression of hunger for the freedom from sin sitting on their faces. Rather, an open arm toward public displays of unnatural relationships. Enter the tool of judgment. Lesson one in how to use this tool for the Kingdom of God: unabashed sin displayed by an unremorseful Christian.

Scripture:

> *Let him who has done this*
> *be removed from among you.*
> *For though absent in body,*
> *I am present in spirit;*
> *and as if present,*
> *I have already pronounced judgment*
> *on the one who did such a thing.*
>
> *When you are assembled*
> *in the name of the Lord Jesus*
> *and my spirit is present,*
> *with the power of our Lord Jesus,*
> *you are to deliver this man to Satan*
> *for the destruction of the flesh,*
> *so that his spirit may be saved*
> *in the day of the Lord.*
> *1 Corinthians 5:2b–5*

I get it. Discussing this matter of sin is the worst. It is the worst when we view it through the awkward conversations that inevitably ensue. It is the worst when we set our eyes on the ease of letting a behavior pass in place of calling it out as what it is—sin. We fear being "judgey." We worry about casting stones. We hide behind a stone wall rather than standing on the solid Rock. What, we wonder, will others think of us if we cast judgment? How, we wonder, will the accused feel about our spewed words? Will they leave our church? Will they spread word about our judgmental manners? Our internal dialogue goes haywire when faced with blatant sin.

What is the solution to silencing this inner dialogue? Jesus.

Paul delivers harsh words in this chapter regarding the sinful relationship accepted within the Corinthian church. Too often, however, we dwell on Paul's harsh words regarding the sexual relationship between a man and his father's wife while skipping over the center point of Paul's words to the Corinthian church, words incredibly useful for you and me today: "When you are assembled in the name of the Lord Jesus...."

New Testament believers unite as saved individuals, don't we? We unite in the name of the very One who saved us — the One who saved us from our sin. Pause for a quick minute. At one point in our individual lives, we found ourselves on our knees seeking private forgiveness from Christ Jesus for our sin. Some of us have proclaimed our sin loud and proud. Others let sin dwell in the Pandora's box we have secretly decorated so well. In both instances, Jesus knows what sin(s) we proclaim sorrow over. He saw us in our heartache over it. He forgave us of our sins. He washed us new in His blood. He stood us on the Rock called Jesus Christ our Lord. From that point on, Christ Jesus, the risen Savior of the world, became our personal and favored Lord of our lives. Oh, how we melt at this truth!

In this freedom of His forgiving love, we unite one with the other to worship His name, to study His Word, to grow in knowledge of Him and to connect as a body of Christ. What does blatant sexual sin between a son and his dad's wife do to your walk in God's forgiving love? Be honest. Be real. How does that affect your walk with the Lord Jesus Christ? Does this man's freedom of choice grow your relationship with the King? Does it hinder you in any way? Does it hinder your children? Raise disconcerting questions at your family's dinner table? Please refrain from seeing this evaluation as judgment. At some point wisdom and truth reign.

When ill behavior is proclaiming itself as normal, it is only wise to view it in truth. It is through evaluation like this, we learn how to use the tool of judgment without casting selfish judgment upon another. Does this make sense? Here is another question to evaluate the next time blatant sin enters your congregation.

Where is Christ during worship? Is He on His Throne or is He on the cross? Truly, consider this with me for a minute. Allow this to break your heart. Jesus blessed those who mourn for our sin.[44] When we are standing in sweet unison with the sole intention of worshipping the King of kings, our love is pouring out at His feet. Our awe at what He has freed us from drips from the depths of our soul. We are in worship to the Savior in our hearts and our souls and our lives.

During this worship, a family member stands there wearing a ragged, filthy coat buried in the likeness of Christ's death that he has dug up and worn yet again. This family member stands there in the stench of decay, wrapped in the cloth of forgiven disdain, walking about as if Jesus were back on the splintered cross. And this person does not care. He raises his hands in worship then wraps his arms around his mother figure with marital admiration. This is gross. It is a heartbreaking scene that brings death back on the empty cross at Calvary.

In fear of judging, we turn a blind eye, throwing our stones at acceptable situations like the actor that has shamed himself publicly, or the professional ballplayer who took the wrong stance, or the unsaved neighbor who did not behave himself quite as Christlike as you did.

Sometimes I do not want to teach. Sometimes I do not want to write.

Scripture:

Your boasting is not good.
Do you not know that a little leaven leavens the whole lump?
Cleanse out the old leaven that you may be a new lump,
as you really are unleavened.

For Christ, our Passover lamb, has been sacrificed.
Let us therefore celebrate the festival,
not with the old leaven, the leaven of malice and evil,
but with the unleavened bread of sincerity and truth.
1 Corinthians 5:6–8

---

[44] Matthew 5:4

Consider the confidence of your non-judgmental acceptance. Are you looking at the whole picture as a painting of love and forgiveness without looking at the colors that created the artwork? Or as Paul pictured it, are you looking at the loaf of bread in its beautifully baked self, or are you considering the ingredients within? How often do we think we are healthy eaters until we look at one more label? We see these words and wonder what we just consumed. Then, sadly, we take another bite. Perhaps we are determined to believe that if it tastes good to our twisted tastebuds that it cannot be all that bad. But deep down we know. Oh, we know. At this point, we have a choice to make. Continue eating that chemical, that sugar, that dye. Or mature a bit and walk away.

Friend, we are all members of one body. We will detail this in the upcoming chapters. Paul frequently compares the body of Christ to the human body to declare the vitality of functioning as one body. The reason for this: It is easily applicable. We all have a body. This is something every single human can relate to. In our human body, we can easily understand the repercussions of wrong choices, right? If we are honest, we could all list the things that fare poorly within our systems. We know that when we make that choice, our bodies will feel the pain or discomfort of it later. From wheat to vodka to high-fructose corn syrup to dairy, our bodies know what they can and cannot process. It is up to us, the soul of the body, to decide whether we want to honor our body or not.

How foolish of us to refrain from listening to the purification needs of our bodies. It is rather silly and kind of selfish of us to neglect ourselves that blatantly. This is Paul's point. Don't you know that we are the body of Christ? Don't you know that a little bit of yeast in a loaf of bread is going to affect the loaf as a whole? Just as our blood streams throughout our entire bodies, so does yeast permeate throughout the entire loaf, so does sin affect the entire body of Christ. The symbolism is undisputable. The reality hurts. The question is: Does our hurt bring us to a mournful spirit or toward a display of acceptance?

Allow me to tie up this inner dialogue with a final thought for you to contemplate. The process of leavening a loaf of bread happens quickly and thoroughly. Much is the same with the allowance of sin (leaven) within the church family. Paul gives us great advice in coming to terms with Biblically-timed acts of judgment. Jesus. It always goes back to Jesus. You will find your answer there every time.

Jesus is the answer in this situation, in this passage. Paul advises the Corinthian believers to go back to the sacrifice. Think about the origin of unleavened bread. Go back to the history of God's people. Go back to the plan of freedom from physical slavery. Go back to the plan of freedom from personal slavery to sin and shame. The plan was the same: the blood of a sacrificial lamb. In our case as New Testament believers, we stand side by side among the Corinthians. As New Testament believers, we remember the sacrifice of the Spotless Lamb. We remember His love displayed on the cross on Calvary. We remember the purity and the kindness and the purpose and the freedom that spilled from the cross upon our sins and upon our eternal separation from God Almighty. We remember Jesus.

Jesus is the source of our beginning, personally and as a body of believers. He is the sincerity and truth on which we stand, in which we worship. He alone is the answer as to what we desire to enter into His body. Jesus.

Scripture:

I wrote to you in my letter
not to associate with sexually immoral people —
not at all meaning the sexually immoral of this world,
or the greedy and swindlers, or idolaters,
since then you would need to go out of the world.

But now I am writing to you
not to associate with anyone who bears the name of brother
if he is guilty of sexual immorality or greed,
or is an idolater, reviler, drunkard, or swindler —
not even to eat with such a one.
1 Corinthians 5:9–11

This is not the first time the Corinthian church struggled with understanding the difference between casting stones of judgment and utilizing the tool of judgment. Nor are they the last Christians who battled with knowing the difference. For you and I are sitting here today attempting to understand this fine line. Paul reminds them that he sent the advice of separation among "sexually immoral people" not to "eat with them" in a previous conversation. Seeing that the topic was still unclear, he added a lengthy description of what he meant.

There is a difference, he says, between the unsaved behaving as the unsaved and a brother/sister who claims the name of Jesus Christ our Lord and behaves as the unsaved. A significant difference.

- One does not know freedom.
- One is choosing to dress in the stench of sin and death while partaking in the freedom found in Christ Jesus.

Let us not be so busy separating ourselves from the unsaved and thereby limiting the light of Jesus Christ upon another man's soul (more on this in Chapter 9). Equally, let us not be so defensive in protecting a Christian, thereby allowing his/her blatant sin to darken the presence of Jesus Christ upon another person's soul. We truly need to build up and protect the body of Christ, just as we need to purpose to build up and protect our individual bodies. What comes inside matters — nourishment or contamination. The choice is ours to make.

When we utilize judgment as a tool of protection toward the body of Christ, we do not apply this in the same manner as casting stones of judgment. We must see the difference. If we don't, we might completely negate the love of Jesus spilled out on the cross. He died for all. He conquered sin for all. He rose again for all. But not everyone knows that. It is our sweet opportunity as the eyes that see Jesus to bring the blind to Christ. How does a child of God proclaim the freedom from sin while we sit in the mud with a Christian who refuses to get out of the mud? It is counterproductive.

Jaclyn Palmer

Scripture:

For what have I to do with judging outsiders?
Is it not those inside the church whom you are to judge?
God judges those outside.
"Purge the evil person from among you."
1 Corinthians 5:12–13

My prayer is that we will take these concluding verses personally, for these words certainly still apply to us today. I pray, as we sit with the truths revealed in this chapter, that we will see it all through the heart of God, that is, the heart of a parent.

It is ever so important to understand that we are not applying this "line of separation" to someone who is unsaved and behaving as someone who is unsaved. In these situations, we meet this person where they are and love them to Jesus. That is settled.

We are not applying this to a brother who is remorseful and is heading back to the "straight and narrow." This brother is choosing Jesus. He is striving to stand yet again. He is seeing his path from the valley to the mountaintop. He is allowing the heart of God to embrace him. This is settled.

We are, however, to display a purposed separation from the brother whose choices disregard the Name we all hold so dearly. This person is in a continuous pattern of sin and would rather pursue this pattern while taking advantage of the protection of the family of God. This person wants both lives. He cannot have both. It is as if we want to sit with popcorn and ice cream all day and desire a fit and healthy physique. We must choose what we genuinely want and pursue it.

Do you hear God's words in Revelation when he tells the church of Laodicea to be either hot or cold? As a living being and as a church family, we must choose hot or cold. One or the other. When we choose to sit in the middle, in the realm of lukewarm, we become a distaste in the mouth of God. I do not want that. I do not want to be cold. I do not want to choose anything that runs away from the arms of God. I do not.

What about you? You must make your choice. And in your choosing, you must protect what you love, not out of judgment, but out of Christ's love. Final thought: The tool of judgment is never used in a self-righteous way but in His righteous way.

Jaclyn Palmer

Notes

1 Corinthians 6

When one of you has a grievance against another, does he dare go to law before the unrighteous instead of the saints? Or do you not know that the saints will judge the world? And if the world is to be judged by you, are you incompetent to try trivial cases? Do you not know that we are to judge angels? How much more, then, matters pertaining to this life! So if you have such cases, why do you lay them before those who have no standing in the church? I say this to your shame. Can it be that there is no one among you wise enough to settle a dispute between the brothers, but brother goes to law against brother, and that before unbelievers? To have lawsuits at all with one another is already a defeat for you. Why not rather suffer wrong? Why not rather be defrauded? But you yourselves wrong and defraud — even your own brothers!

Or do you not know that the unrighteous will not inherit the kingdom of God? Do not be deceived: neither the sexually immoral, nor idolaters, nor adulterers, nor men who practice homosexuality, nor thieves, nor the greedy, nor drunkards, nor revilers, nor swindlers will inherit the kingdom of God. And such were some of you. But you were washed, you were sanctified, you were justified in the name of the Lord Jesus Christ and by the Spirit of our God.

"All things are lawful for me," but not all things are helpful. "All things are lawful for me," but I will not be dominated by anything. "Food is meant for the stomach and the stomach for food" — and God will destroy both one and the other. The body is not meant for sexual immorality, but for the Lord, and the Lord for the body. And God raised the Lord and will also raise us up by his power. Do you not know that your bodies are members of Christ? Shall I then take the members of Christ and make them members of a prostitute? Never!

Jaclyn Palmer

Or do you not know that he who is joined to a prostitute becomes one body with her? For, as it is written, "The two will become one flesh." But he who is joined to the Lord becomes one spirit with him. Flee from sexual immorality. Every other sin a person commits is outside the body, but the sexually immoral person sins against his own body. Or do you not know that your body is a temple of the Holy Spirit within you, whom you have from God? You are not your own, for you were bought with a price. So glorify God in your body.

6

The Place of Judgment

But you were washed,
you were sanctified,
you were justified
in the name of the Lord Jesus Christ
and by the Spirit of our God.
1 Corinthians 6:11b

This chapter in the Bible is interesting, both in its placement and in its context. Last chapter, we discussed the area of sexual immorality within the church family, and next chapter, we will discuss the roles of various marriage statuses. Then this little chapter sits right in between with an equal blend of lawsuits and sexual immorality. Basically, a lot is going on regarding judgment topics. Most center on matters of sexual behaviors with a small rabbit trail of legal matters. At times like this, I wish I had copies of the letters written to Paul to which he is responding.

As an onlooker, I wonder why so much discussion occurs on such "obvious" topics. However, this is when we have to step aside to consider the habits of Corinth. Perhaps with a side observation of cable TV. Perhaps. To start, Paul enters the courtroom.

Scripture:

> *When one of you has a grievance against another,*
> *does he dare go to law before the unrighteous*
> *instead of the saints?*
> *1 Corinthians 6:1*

Legal matters have been a topic of advice since the days of Moses. Do you remember when he was leading the Israelites through the wilderness and judging every legal matter simultaneously?[45] Have you ever been in a room of kindergarteners? We have much to compare. God called and equipped Moses to lead the Israelites out of Egypt and into Canaan. This was his job that came with thousands upon thousands of followers — unhappy, discontented followers. In the midst of talking to God, leading the thousands, scouting maps and byways, and conquering his personal issues of insecurity and irritable nature, he was spending hours each day settling disputes.

Enter his father-in-law. Through Jethro's wisdom, he kindly offered sound life skills to his son-in-law. For free. He willingly instructed Moses how to lead, how to delegate, and how to focus on what he needed to accomplish. Moses had a choice at that moment. Scripture tells us that he decided to listen with a teachable spirit. He opted to put this newfound lesson to practice. So, rather than single handedly leading thousands upon thousands of people, he led a handful. Allowing the handful the opportunity to step up in leadership and responsibility is wisdom.

Here we are in the days of Corinth seeing the need for legal advice yet again. The main question: "Who is settling your disputes?" As we read Paul's words, we see how deeply he feels on this matter and why.

Scripture:

> *Or do you not know that the saints will judge the world?*
> *And if the world is to be judged by you,*

---

[45] Exodus 18

are you incompetent to try trivial cases?
Do you not know that we are to judge angels?
How much more, then, matters pertaining to this life!
So if you have such cases,
why do you lay them before those
who have no standing in the church?
1 Corinthians 6:2–4

What he feels is solid conviction that legal matters between the family of God ought to remain within the family of God. Why? Because we, as the heirs to the Throne, have the position of righteous judgment. God has called His children to judge matters with justice and truth. He is equipping us to one day judge angels. We are the children of God Almighty, having the mind of Jesus Christ and filled with the Holy Spirit. How can we not settle our own family matters?

This truth is unfamiliar to some of us, is it not? This truth stubs some toes. We may have been to court over civil matters. Some of us have taken our personal heartaches before a judge seeking a verdict that will soothe our pain and heal our wounds.

I remember being in a prison waiting room to spend time with someone my little-girl heart loved. I recall a lawyer asking questions about my mom's soon-to-be second husband who wanted me to take on his last name as my own. I remember the judge who settled the case, feelings and emotions swirling…. Words trapped within me. Uncertain as to what I was supposed to feel. Whom was I supposed to love "more"? Wondering why I was not enough for others to love.

Legal matters are tough. They come with hard truths, solid lies, and unwanted confusion. Hearts are often broken. The innocent all too often caught in the middle. Sorrow is typically the outcome. Overall, legal matters are bound to happen. They have occurred since the dawn of the first generation when two sons ended up as the suspect and the victim of the first murder scene. Legal issues spill throughout the Old Testament, hence the above passage regarding Moses, the book of Judges, and the chronicles of the kings. And we are more than aware that they continue to happen today.

Legal matters happen because of our broken world and inborn sin nature. These two things combined create matters too big for our hearts to comprehend. Add the determination of Satan to the mix, and quite literally, it feels like all hell has broken loose.

The emotions tied to this passage are daunting. This chapter may not be able to rectify the damage through which you have already lived. To this truth, I am so deeply sorry for the hurt and the angst this portion of our study may have caused you. But you can allow its truth to guide your steps today, mixed with the wisdom you have attained through yesterday, and proceed into tomorrow with a little more clarity.

Scripture:

*Can it be that there is no one among you
wise enough to settle
a dispute between the brothers,
but brother goes to law against brother,
and that before unbelievers?
To have lawsuits at all with one another
is already a defeat for you.
Why not rather suffer wrong?
Why not rather be defrauded?
But you yourselves wrong and defraud —
even your own brothers!
1 Corinthians 6:5b–8*

Two specific truths are ours to use as stepping stones of clarity, to settle a dispute and to beat defeat. Ultimately, we need to see it before it blows up. Approach the smallest of matters before it escalates into something larger. Perhaps we need to finetune the larger situation to see the smaller matter to settle that dispute before it grows more. The key is to look further than what you see right in front of you.

I am curious if a passage of Scripture is pressing on your heart as you read that last paragraph? As I was writing it, Matthew 7:3 coursed through my mind. "Mind your log before you go after their speck." (my translation) I am aware of the power of this truth in relation to settling a dispute. I have been married for 21 years. I am raising a teenage son. I have been a part of ministry throughout my life. I have an extensive list of girlfriends. A have seen disputes in each of these relationships. Humans dispute. It is going to happen. What does not have to happen is defeat. To disallow defeat, we must see each minor dispute for what it is. This takes work and constant awareness. Also, honest self-evaluation. Is it possible in any stretch of the imagination that the log in your eye[46] caused the dispute?

To settle a dispute among yourselves is honorable; and, friend, it is attainable. The presence of Jesus in your heart, the Spirit alive within you, and God on His Throne will help you. May we purpose — each and every day, every moment — to recall these three truths. May we etch them in our minds, write them on our mirrors, post them on our screens. Jesus is here. The Spirit is here. God is here. See it. Feel it. Walk in it. Speak in it. Respond in it. Be the evidence of it. Not because you are faking and trying to but because He is, and you are His. Proceed in His presence day by day, moment by moment, victory by victory, strength by strength; and then breathe.

In purposing to settle the dispute, instantly and at its core, you are staying a step ahead of defeat. Does this make you smile in His freedom? Does it make you feel like you have a game plan to stand on? Can you feel His armor covering you?[47] Do you see each dispute as an opportunity for victory? I pray you do!

We felt the weight of our past failure as we sat to study this passage. Defeat is a reality. But as we said earlier, we may need to use yesterday's defeat as today's homework for tomorrow's victory.

---

[46] Matthew 7:3
[47] Ephesians 6:10–20

We can stay ahead of defeat if we know how to fight and when we understand whom we are to fight.

Scripture:

> *Or do you not know that the unrighteous*
> *will not inherit the kingdom of God?*
> *Do not be deceived:*
> *neither the sexually immoral,*
> *nor idolaters, nor adulterers,*
> *nor men who practice homosexuality,*
> *nor thieves, nor the greedy,*
> *nor drunkards, nor revilers,*
> *nor swindlers will inherit the kingdom of God.*
> *And such were some of you.*
>
> *But you were washed,*
> *you were sanctified, you were justified*
> *in the name of the Lord Jesus Christ*
> *and by the Spirit of our God.*
> *1 Corinthians 6:9–11*

Do you recognize this list from the last chapter? We are not foolish enough to believe that the unsaved are the only ones to portray these sins. At times, a Christian chooses to walk in one of these sins (or one that is outside this list). 1 Corinthians Chapter 5 takes us through the process of judging the saved in this situation. Furthermore, the first half of this chapter sits with us in our processing of how to proceed when the sin of others turns into a legal heartache. This is the habit of sin, is it not? It starts as a thought but crosses a line that becomes too big to contain.

Personal note of motivation: Do not feed a thought. Settle that internal thought on the spot. Quote Scripture aloud the moment a thought tries to overtake you. Pray the Name of Jesus Christ aloud. See Jesus with you, feel the Spirit within you, declare that God is on His Throne! Defeat that thought before it grows into a sin that easily defeats you or one you love.

In relation to dealing with the sin of an unsaved person when it affects your personal life, proceed with caution. At times, when dealing with an unsaved person, legal action is both needed and encouraged. Protect yourself. Protect the innocence of children who are at risk of harm. Too often, in fear of not wanting to disobey this passage regarding legal cases outside of the body of Christ, we remain in our story, or we allow ourselves to become a doormat in the name of Jesus. May I delicately say this is not benefiting anything? You can proclaim the name of Christ in self-defense, in strength, in taking a stand for purity and freedom. In fact, the depth of the strength of our Lord is so much greater than the ill display of weak submission. Is that fair for me to say?

Before proceeding to the second topic of 1 Corinthians 6, may I whisper something into your heart? You are not responsible for everyone's salvation. God has rightfully claimed that role. Perhaps — the hungry soul watching to see Jesus in you is not the person you are trying to save. Sometimes we are so careful to lead one person to the Lord that we put up with wrongful doings that are causing more harm than eternal good. Sweet friend, may I encourage you to look around you to see who else is watching your situation? I pray you will be mindful of that person's soul as well.

There are multiple levels and various situations that erupt in a topic such as this. My prayer is that this Scripture study will be a stepping stone to your finding His freedom in your situation. Xo

Scripture:

> *"All things are lawful for me,"*
> *but not all things are helpful.*
> *"All things are lawful for me,"*
> *but I will not be dominated by anything.*
> *"Food is meant for the stomach*
> *and the stomach for food" —*
> *and God will destroy both one and the other.*

The body is not meant for sexual immorality,
but for the Lord,
and the Lord for the body.
And God raised the Lord
and will also raise us up by his power.
1 Corinthians 6:12–14

So, what if others are righteously judging us? What if the tables turn? What if we neglect this portion of Scripture and press on in our sweet journey of learning how to judge *others* instead? Oh boy, sometimes Scripture gets real, doesn't it? Shall we get real with Scripture? Are you in? If not, I will see you in the second half of Chapter 11—that is the sweetest portion of this entire journey.

So, there we are in our freedom in Christ, and a friend approaches us with the judgment of sincerity and truth. Paul gives us six sentences in verses 12 and 13 that we can consider. I encourage us to process these statements before the righteous judgment comes at us, again. Three sentences justify our truths; three sentences proclaim His truth.

Please remember, there are times, as seen in Chapter 3, that judgment will come to us by righteous people but in an unrighteous way or via their naivety. Be real in assessing the judgment without judging the judger. However, there may be a time when we behave in a manner that emulates sin. Maybe. Perhaps it is possible that our flesh overtakes us at a moment's notice. Let us be willing to receive the righteous words of a friend or a member of the body of Christ.

- All things are lawful for me.
- All things are lawful for me.
- Food is meant for the stomach and the stomach is meant for food.

Funny how easily our justifications repeat themselves. We have said them and heard them so often that we fail to hear the amusing cycle of repetition. As if we cannot produce a better quip to silence the Spirit within us. I suppose it is at the point that we master a better line that sin becomes rooted within us, and lines become crossed in our hearts and actions. With that said, good for us for being so redundant and unoriginal in our determination to pout as we justify sin.

Odds are the actions called out are legal for us. Odds are we are old enough and independent and human enough to be doing this matter held in "court." Odds are it is natural, as well. The thing we are putting in our bodies is a natural craving of our bodies. We know this is truth; therefore, it is that easy to justify. If these three sentences are lighting an internal fight within your soul, will you jump ahead to Chapter 9? Spend time there. Then come back and see this passage anew.

If you are taking this in stride, will you ponder the heart behind these statements? Are they worth it? The arguments that ensue. The inevitable dispute that is knocking at the door. The defeat that is waiting around the corner. Is it worth claiming "It's lawful. It's natural!" when peace and ease and freedom are sitting on the other side of the table? I am simply asking that we consider this before the next situation arises.

To take this personal evaluation even deeper, if you have a conviction pressed on your heart from the Lord, will you set your justifications aside in order to press forward to the prize that He desires to award you? I guarantee that the reward of obedience and trust will run circles around that thing you are justifying.

- Not all things are helpful.
- I will not allow anything to dominate me.
- God will destroy both food and the stomach.

Interesting how peacefully God's truth can silence our inner pout while building us up with strength and determination. It is almost as if, once we pull out these proclaimed truths, the entire passage makes perfect sense. It helps us see our participation in legal pursuits. It enables us to take a step back in wrongfully judging and righteously judging those around us. It strengthens us in our personal defense to pursue a higher calling in life. And it frees us from the cyclical self-bondage of justification.

Truth. It will set us free.[48] Who knew?

Scripture:

> *But he who is joined to the Lord*
> *becomes one spirit with him.*
> *Or do you not know that your body*
> *is a temple of the Holy Spirit within you,*
> *whom you have from God?*
> *You are not your own,*
> *for you were bought with a price.*
> *So glorify God in your body.*
> *1 Corinthians 6:17 & 19*

What a powerful Scripture to claim and proclaim as we conclude the last two chapters of sin. Do you know whose you are? Do you believe that He cares truly for your well-being and for the protection of your body inside and out? Do you know that you are His?

In that knowledge, may we grow in freedom from the sin or the behavior that can lead to a defiant sin within us (pride, selfishness, stubbornness, etcetera) so that we can grow in the freedom of Christ's ever presence in us, around us, and through us.

---

[48] John 8:31-36

Notes

Jaclyn Palmer

1 Corinthians 7

Now concerning the matters about which you wrote: "It is good for a man not to have sexual relations with a woman." But because of the temptation to sexual immorality, each man should have his own wife and each woman her own husband. The husband should give to his wife her conjugal rights, and likewise the wife to her husband. For the wife does not have authority over her own body, but the husband does. Likewise the husband does not have authority over his own body, but the wife does. Do not deprive one another, except perhaps by agreement for a limited time, that you may devote yourselves to prayer; but then come together again, so that Satan may not tempt you because of your lack of self-control.

Now as a concession, not a command, I say this. I wish that all were as I myself am. But each has his own gift from God, one of one kind and one of another.

To the unmarried and the widows I say that it is good for them to remain single, as I am. But if they cannot exercise self-control, they should marry. For it is better to marry than to burn with passion.

To the married I give this charge (not I, but the Lord): the wife should not separate from her husband (but if she does, she should remain unmarried or else be reconciled to her husband), and the husband should not divorce his wife.

To the rest I say (I, not the Lord) that if any brother has a wife who is an unbeliever, and she consents to live with him, he should not divorce her. If any woman has a husband who is an unbeliever, and he consents to live with her, she should not divorce him. For the unbelieving husband is made holy because of his wife, and the unbelieving wife is made holy because of her husband.

*Otherwise your children would be unclean, but as it is, they are holy.
But if the unbelieving partner separates, let it be so. In such cases the
brother or sister is not enslaved. God has called you to peace. For how
do you know, wife, whether you will save your husband? Or how do
you know, husband, whether you will save your wife?*

*Only let each person lead the life that the Lord has assigned to him, and to
which God has called him. This is my rule in all the churches. Was anyone
at the time of his call already circumcised? Let him not seek to remove the
marks of circumcision. Was anyone at the time of his call uncircumcised?
Let him not seek circumcision. For neither circumcision counts for anything
nor uncircumcision, but keeping the commandments of God. Each one should
remain in the condition in which he was called. Were you a bondservant
when called? Do not be concerned about it. (But if you can gain your freedom,
avail yourself of the opportunity.) For he who was called in the Lord
as a bondservant is a freedman of the Lord. Likewise he who was free when
called is a bondservant of Christ. You were bought with a price; do not
become bondservants of men. So, brothers, in whatever condition
each was called, there let him remain with God.*

*Now concerning the betrothed, I have no command from the Lord, but I
give my judgment as one who by the Lord's mercy is trustworthy. I think
that in view of the present distress it is good for a person to remain as he is.
Are you bound to a wife? Do not seek to be free. Are you free from a wife?
Do not seek a wife. But if you do marry, you have not sinned, and if a betrothed
woman marries, she has not sinned. Yet those who marry will have worldly
troubles, and I would spare you that. This is what I mean, brothers:
the appointed time has grown very short. From now on, let those who have
wives live as though they had none, and those who mourn as though they
were not mourning, and those who rejoice as though they were not rejoicing,
and those who buy as though they had no goods, and those who deal
with the world as though they had no dealings with it.
For the present form of this world is passing away.*

Jaclyn Palmer

*I want you to be free from anxieties. The unmarried man is anxious about
the things of the Lord, how to please the Lord. But the married man
is anxious about worldly things, how to please his wife, and his interests
are divided. And the unmarried or betrothed woman is anxious about
the things of the Lord, how to be holy in body and spirit. But the married
woman is anxious about worldly things, how to please her husband.
I say this for your own benefit, not to lay any restraint upon you,
but to promote good order and to secure your undivided devotion to the Lord.*

*If anyone thinks that he is not behaving properly toward his betrothed, if
his passions are strong, and it has to be, let him do as he wishes: let them
marry — it is no sin. But whoever is firmly established in his heart, being under
no necessity but having his desire under control, and has determined this in his
heart, to keep her as his betrothed, he will do well. So then he who marries his
betrothed does well, and he who refrains from marriage will do even better.*

*A wife is bound to her husband as long as he lives. But if her husband dies,
she is free to be married to whom she wishes, only in the Lord.
Yet in my judgment she is happier if she remains as she is.
And I think that I too have the Spirit of God.*

7

As You Are, Contentedly

Now concerning matters about which you wrote:
"It is good for a man not to have sexual relations with a woman."
1 Corinthians 7:1

Now. Now that we have learned how to differentiate between casting judgment and utilizing proper judgment within the body of Christ, it is time to tread sweetly into Chapter 7 with a unified vision rather than a soapbox of division. How freeing is that?

This chapter sitting before us is a wonderful opportunity to put what we have learned into practice. For some, we will be practicing how to discern our own marital status through the eyes of God rather than in the temptation of judging ourselves. Some of us will drop our stones of judgment upon the marriages of others. We do this, don't we? We critique situations that we do not fully understand. And by critique, you know, I mean judge. Others of us will be able to simply sit back and grow in connection with God and with our circle of friends knowing that we have found the freedom in this area of marriage, divorce, singleness, judgment, and healing—knowing that each situation is unique in its personal walk with God Almighty.

Jaclyn Palmer

Scripture:

Now concerning the matters about which you wrote:
"It is good for a man not to have sexual relations with a woman."
But because of the temptation to sexual immorality,
each man should have his own wife
and each woman her own husband.
The husband should give to his wife her conjugal rights,
and likewise the wife to her husband.
For the wife does not have authority
over her own body, but the husband does.
Likewise the husband does not have authority
over his own body, but the wife does.
Do not deprive one another,
except perhaps by agreement for a limited time,
that you may devote yourselves to prayer;
but then come together again,
so that Satan may not tempt you
because of your lack of self-control.
1 Corinthians 7:1–5

Now. Now Paul addresses an extremely specific issue presented to him by the same people that brought up the issue of accepting blatant sin in their church. Interesting how difficult it was for the first-century Christians to grasp what it looked like to be a follower of Jesus Christ. So much new mingled with existing old. All things Jesus was new and applicable in every area of life. Yet the city, the surroundings, the culture, the setting, the traditions, the flesh, the devil, the broken world were all still present, still pulling at them.

Then they brought the matter of sex to the table. As they openly accepted the decay in Chapter 5, they simultaneously cast a law upon one another that is not in agreement with the written Word. They say, "It is good for a man not to have sexual relations with a woman." Side note: People often credit Paul for this statement considering his highly opinionated view of remaining single. However, he deflected this statement with the gift of marriage that God instituted, created, and gifted to all who receive it. Let us not blame Paul for this man-made law.

For, this man-made law only leads to sexual sin. For human nature declares, "I cannot; therefore, I must." Case in point: every diet every Monday morning.

Paul, despite his vote for remaining single, opens this chapter with his defense of God's plan for marriage. In fact, he states powerful points on marriage that we must not overlook.

- Proper marriage is the obvious answer to deflect sexual temptation.
- Proper marriage is a united platform to equally say, "Yes."
- Prayer is your only out.

When it comes to marriage, I feel like Paul's little sister standing on her tip toes declaring, "Nuh-uh!" to everything he says. Well, not everything, but his "don't get married things." When I hear negativity spilling out of wives regarding marriage, I feel like shouting truths from the bottom of a love-filled heart. And it is not simply because of my marriage, but it is because I have seen the fails and the wins of marriage. I have seen the brokenness and healing. I have seen unity and division. And I passionately believe that marriage is on the top of Satan's list to destroy. He hates this gift that God created for Adam and Eve and for you and for me.

Satan's first presence on earth was with the intent of separating man from God and man from his wife. Why? What is in marriage that is a personal attack on Satan? Why does he hate it so desperately? Because the image of marriage is a beautiful symbolism of our personal relationship with God Almighty through the love displayed by Jesus Christ on the cross at Calvary.

It is not just love. It is the very personal love of our Creator, God who reigns on the Throne as the King. Lucifer takes the very design of marriage as a thorn in the side of his selfish nature. Therefore, he will play all his redundant cards to destroy the institution of marriage. Every time!

95

Sweet sister, Satan is so incredibly backward. He desires little more than to twist this area of right and wrong, of sex and marriage, of purity and love. He wants us to blame society, for blame is in our sin nature born at the time of his first attack. But there is nothing new in our society that has not been in all of the societies of every era. The damage is Satan's. That is not blame; that is truth! It all started with a piece of fruit. The moment Eve and Adam took a bite, just a bite, of the fruit from the tree of the knowledge of good and evil, their eyes were immediately opened. Opened to what? Good and evil.

The problem is this: Good and evil in the eyes of God vary from good and evil in the eyes of mankind. When Eve and Adam saw through their new vision, their first sight was of their own nudity. Why? Why wasn't their first vision of the fruit? Or the snake? Or the tree, for that matter — the very source that bore the fruit? Why did their eyes immediately go inward and toward one another? In response to their new vision Adam said, "I was afraid, because I was naked, and I hid myself." [49] Then they both passed the blame.

Adam, when asked first, because he was the one God had told not to eat from the tree, blamed God for giving him the woman; Eve blamed the serpent who tricked her. They passed the blame as they stood side by side covering their skin with leaves. How long, I wonder, did that take? Picking out the right leaves, figuring out how to connect them, which pattern would best cover their bodies — because you know, men's hips vary greatly from female's hips — it's a totally different fit and style. The number of brand-new emotions that must have flowed through them breaks my heart for them. They single-handedly robbed themselves of perfect freedom.

Corruption birthed within the sweet gift of sex and marriage. Guilt, shame, insecurity, and uncertainty became part of their physical existence, and in that, we were born.

---

[49] Genesis 3:9–13

Nudity and sex and marriage were three things created by God in perfect unity. Coverings, shame, and secrecy were born upon the vision of evil. Nudity, sex, and marriage are not the problem. I know that I do not know your body image, and I do not know the issues in your marriage. I do know they are not the problem. God created such gifts in perfection for you and your spouse. Period. See that. The problem is the covering that we hand-stitch together to hide ourselves from God.

Friend, that covering is not covering anything. You cannot hide anything from God. It only looks like a parka on a hot, summer day. That shame that you are holding onto is not okay. I get it. I locked mine in a prized Pandora's box like no one's business. And when it popped open without my consent, I was scared out of my mind. Ten years later, I stood taller, stronger, and freer than ever before. Overcoming shame is not easy. There are steps and processes of forward and backward remembering, forgiving, and letting go. Use this for wisdom by declaring truth in its place and learning to be a new you. It is an exhaustion that precedes an exhilaration. And, friend, whatever secret you are holding from your spouse is poison. It does not matter if it is a $168 receipt from an online purchase or the purposed dreams of adultery with the guy from the gym. It is nasty. It is poison. You must proclaim it, air it out, and throw it away.

Being married is a gift from God. If you are married, BE married. Fully. Embrace it, live it, love it, invest in it, gain from it, make it what you want it to be. Do your part! Same goes for being single. Paul says that being single is the way to live. He was the poster child for all things single, so he advocated for all of us to follow in that service-led dream of a life. I, on the other hand, love being married. So, I humbly advocate for all marriages to be happy. Truly, happy together.

Wherever you are on the marriage spectrum, be happy. Be you. And shine!

Scripture:

> *Only let each person lead the life*
> *that the Lord has assigned to him,*

and to which God has called him.
This is my rule in all the churches.
Was anyone at the time of his call already circumcised?
Let him not seek to remove the marks of circumcision.
Was anyone at the time of his call uncircumcised?
Let him not seek circumcision.
For neither circumcision counts for anything nor uncircumcision,
but keeping the commandments of God.
1 Corinthians 7:17–19

So often we consume our thoughts with what we should be or what our life is supposed to be or what we dream our life could be. In the truth of this passage found in verses 17-24, we see that we already are. We are already living the life that surrounds us. Perhaps there is a religious background that you are not thrilled to be associated with after finding the true love of Christ. Perhaps you are confronted with the reality of the unsaved life you lived before receiving the love of Jesus. Maybe your occupation limits your hours of service to the King, or you do not have a job and need a job. In the meantime, you have hours above measure to worship the Lord.

Here is the heart of Paul's message: Good.

Good, he says. Be where you are. Jesus Christ came to seek and to save the lost where we are. He does not come and whisk us into our next stage of life. Rather, He imparts within us wisdom and knowledge and understanding. He gives us the mind of Christ and the Spirit of God — where we are. Therefore, where we are *in Him* is now where we ought to be. Not to remain for the rest of time. It is where we are starting our journey in Christ. Learn of Him right now. Study and pray and walk and talk and live and shine right now. It is imperative that the light of Jesus Christ grows from 0 to 100 in you where you are. Why? For those around you to see the change that occurs when one receives Jesus Christ as Savior. Your very life becomes a testament of His love — where you are. In this growing process, you learn to embrace Christ's fullness, and you will begin seeing the Spirit's evidential fruit pour out of your life. This will draw you closer to your God. You will grow more by witnessing the growth that is happening.

May I encourage you to reread this passage with a sense of contentment? Not satisfied with the surroundings, but the contentment of your focus on God in the midst of your situation. Don't worry about your past, don't worry about your future, and don't worry about those around you. Remain where you are in the Lord. He will meet you where you are.

You see, it is rarely about the surroundings, the situations, or the circumstances. It is you, and it is God, and it is precious.

Scripture:

> *Now concerning the betrothed,*
> *I have no command from the Lord,*
> *but I give my judgment*
> *as one who by the Lord's mercy is trustworthy.*
> *I think that in view of the present distress*
> *it is good for a person to remain as he is.*
> *Are you bound to a wife?*
> *Do not seek to be free.*
> *Are you free from a wife?*
> *Do not seek a wife.*
>
> *But if you do marry, you have not sinned,*
> *and if a betrothed woman marries,*
> *she has not sinned.*
> *Yet those who marry will have worldly troubles,*
> *and I would spare you that.*
> *1 Corinthians 7:25–28*

Now. Now regarding the Corinthians' question about those who are single, Paul circles back to the beginning of this chapter. Ultimately, have self-control and find joy in singlehood. To be single is to live fully enamored with God. The devotion to a spouse is not battling within you.

This is the prime of life, Paul says. This is the time in life to live for God, fully. His thoughts on marriage are pretty straight forward regardless of the situation behind the question. Do not do it or do it, but whichever you choose, do it wholeheartedly as unto God.

That is great advice.

This passage is a double-sided coin. Hear me out. Paul's greatest desire is that we grasp the joy of living a life undivided for the kingdom of God. This is grand. This is good. God's first gift to us was the gift of marriage so that we can grasp the joy of living a life in the Spirit of God. This is good in the eyes of God Almighty.

Paul writes for himself a time or two to the Corinthians. He writes as a brother in the joy of his personal experience. This is sweet and real of him. I also appreciate that he circles his reality with the words of Truth. That is a good mentor. I pray we will read this chapter in that light. May we drop any stones of judgment that may have his name written on them. Right? Some of us have been dreading this chapter due to the heartache with which we are all too familiar. He is not throwing judgment at the Corinthians or at you. Please do not throw stones at him or at me. The Corinthians asked valid questions. Isn't it interesting how similar their questions are to our culture today? We think we are the only ones in a hard marriage or who desire to be married or who are married to an unbelieving spouse. Maybe—we are simply confused with what marriage is supposed to look like.[50] But we are not alone. You are not alone.

Life is a gift designed by God for each of us. Living is the fruit that spills from His gift of life.

May we stop to reflect on the gift of life and the fruit of our living today? May we see our truth in the light of it being a gift? May we offer our present "living" to the Lord? May we ask Him to walk with us and

---

[50] Ephesians 5:22–33

before us? May we seek to do our part in living fully in the marriage or the singleness in which we find ourselves today?

Sweet friend, there are reasons to seek an escape from the life of singleness and of marriage. There are those who desire to harm, hurt, abuse, cheat on, etcetera. Exceptions exist for behaviors that are in violation to the sanctity of marriage and of life itself.[51] Do not seek Biblical contentment in a life coupled with physical, sexual, or emotional abuse.[52] Does this make sense? God values your life; pursue safety.[53]

---

[51] Deuteronomy 24:1–4; Matthew 19:8; 1 Corinthians 7:15
[52] Exodus 22:22–24; Isaiah 10:1–4; 1 Thessalonians 4:3–8
[53] Psalm 127, 147; John 10

Notes

1 Corinthians 8

Now concerning food offered to idols: we know that "all of us possess knowledge." This "knowledge" puffs up, but love builds up. If anyone imagines that he knows something, he does not yet know as he ought to know. But if anyone loves God, he is known by God.

Therefore, as to the eating of food offered to idols, we know that "an idol has no real existence," and that "there is no God but one." For although there may be so-called gods in heaven or on earth — as indeed there are many "gods" and many "lords" — yet for us there is one God, the Father, from whom are all things and for whom we exist, and one Lord, Jesus Christ, through whom are all things and through whom we exist.

However, not all possess this knowledge. But some, through former association with idols, eat food as really offered to an idol, and their conscience, being weak, is defiled. Food will not commend us to God. We are no worse off if we do not eat, and no better off if we do. But take care that this right of yours does not somehow become a stumbling block to the weak. For if anyone sees you who have knowledge eating in an idol's temple, will he not be encouraged, if his conscience is weak, to eat food offered to idols? And so by your knowledge this weak person is destroyed, the brother for whom Christ died. Thus, sinning against your brothers and wounding their conscience when it is weak, you sin against Christ. Therefore, if food makes my brother stumble, I will never eat meat, lest I make my brother stumble.

Jaclyn Palmer

8

United in His Knowledge

Now concerning food offered to idols:
1 Corinthians 8:1a

N ow. Do you ever feel like we have this chapter all wrong? It is almost as if Paul wrote this chapter with the pure intent to trap us into the realm of guilt. As if anything we do will prohibit another soul from ever learning of the love of God. This mentality washes out the heart of Paul's response to yet another of the Corinthians' questions.

These new believers were trying to process the "rules" of eating and drinking. Paul responds with understanding. He answers them in the situation in which they worded their question. He instructs according to their reality, their mentality. I pray we will remember the lessons of Corinth while wisely responding to the pull of the Spirit within our own realities and mentalities.

As we read this chapter together, will you keep this one jewel in mind? This chapter is less about food, freedom, or stumbling blocks and more about God. God loves you. You know this; you love this truth. Now, let us live it.

Scripture:

> *We know that "all of us possess knowledge."*
> *This "knowledge" puffs up, but love builds up.*
> *If anyone imagines that he knows something,*
> *he does not yet know as he ought to know.*
> *But if anyone loves God, he is known by God.*
> *Therefore, as to the eating of food offered to idols,*
> *we know that "an idol has no real existence,"*
> *and that "there is no God but one."*
> *However, not all possess this knowledge.*
> *1 Corinthians 8:2–4,7a*

Knowledge is wonderful and good. Have knowledge and grow in it. We all like to know things. As we look into this passage, we see that the Corinthians needed to know things: like knowing that nothing permeates into meat making it holy or defiled once offered to an idol. Know things that are useful, practical, and good. But do not merely know all the things. Knowledge is for self. If all you do is grow your knowledge, then all you will do is benefit your own walk. We tend to get all puffed up in our knowledge. Let us not be *that* person.

Paul says to use your knowledge as the strong Christian you are for the benefit of others. The question then remains, how do we turn our internal knowledge to the benefit of those around us?

- Step one: Listen to the Holy Spirit.
- Step two: Be aware of your audience.
- Step three: Live fully in step one and step two.

I did not fully know the Holy Spirit until I became an adult. I mean, I knew my memory verses about the Holy Spirit, and I won all the Bible quiz questions regarding the doctrine of the Holy Spirit. But I did not know how to trust the sweet, personal words of the Spirit until my adult years.

Knowing how to trust the Holy Spirit when He whispers a thought upon your heart is the momentous change that we see in 1 Corinthians 8. This is how we live out this passage without the guilt and weight of being responsible for the souls of all people at all times. This removes the wearing of God's shoes and replaces it with the freedom of the Holy Spirit.

All things are made *by* God and *for* God.[54] In Jesus Christ we live and love. And, Friend, it is through the presence of the Holy Spirit that we are free to live and love fully for God. Then the Holy Spirit whispers within us, and our hearts skip a beat at the presence of Him — we obey. Do not worry about His request being your new way of life or your forever conviction. Simply focus on Him. That one moment, that one whisper is not about you or your knowledge or your strength or your weakness or your liberty to live in freedom. Nor is it about the Scripture that advises us to refrain from being "a stumbling block." His request for you in that moment is bigger than you.

Often, that single whisper in that one moment from the Holy Spirit to you, His precious daughter, is for someone else around you.

Whether you are aware of the situation or not, trust that the Spirit is using you in that moment to reveal Himself to others where they are. How beautiful to know that in our simple trust and obedience to the voice of the Spirit, another soul can draw closer to God. This is a powerful, humble truth.

Scripture:

> *For although there may be so-called gods*
> *in heaven or on earth —*
> *as indeed there are many "gods"*
> *and many "lords" — yet for us*
> *there is one God, the Father,*
> *from whom are all things*

---

[54] John 1:3; Colossians 1:16

> *and for whom we exist,*
> *and one Lord, Jesus Christ,*
> *through whom are all things*
> *and through whom we exist.*
> *1 Corinthians 8:5–6*

The placement of this precious truth is more than powerful; it is needful. For if we are going to grasp the vitality of putting the voice of the Spirit above ourselves, it is imperative that we have our purest knowledge wrapped around the truest source of knowledge. God the Father, and Jesus Christ the Son, have created all things, and they have created all things for their glory and pleasure and will.

There is such a loving depth in the simple statements penned in verse six. God is the heart behind all things and all people. Grasp that truth. All things and all people get their function and purpose and breath from God the Father. That includes the liquid you are sipping right now, the food you are picking at while reading this chapter, and it includes you. All things and all people are from God and for God.

The truth stacks higher as Paul pens, "Jesus Christ, through whom are all things and through whom we exist." We have life because He has life. His life was from the beginning. His life was lived out in the flesh. His life, crucified and offered up, was the final sacrifice for all people who are from God and for God. His life was resurrected from the dead. His life was and is and is to come. We have that life when we have Jesus Christ. That, my friend, is a depth-packed simple statement. I encourage you to pause for a moment and ponder the depth of His life in you and through you for His purpose and His will.

This chapter in Corinthians has always been a hard chapter for me. It felt like a well built around me in which others poured buckets of guilt and shame, drowning me in the weight of law and restriction, of behavior and stumbling blocks, of weakness and strength. It was all consuming and suffocating. This well was an attempt to conform me to the image of another. Not Jesus, another. Another man, another conviction, another reputation, another jesus. This is not Scriptural. It is quite the opposite of the very promise of Christ as the place of rest seen in Matthew 11.

In 1 Corinthians 8, we learn freedom from the weight of obligation, and it calls us to walk in the Spirit with attention on the audience before us. It teaches truth in accordance with the teaching of Jesus Christ. It communicates the love of God for you and for the one near you. And it lays down the beauty of a life lived in the fullness of the Holy Spirit. I see this now. And I smile. The very chapter that constrained me for years is the very chapter that frees me to listen and to live. I pray the constraint from others will dissipate, and the freedom to listen and to live will be the life that sustains in you and through you for His glory.

Scripture:

> *However, not all possess this knowledge....*
> *1 Corinthians 8:7a*

May this one sentence be the thought that secures our next decision in equal freedom and love. We know that all things and all people are from and for God. We know that all things and all people are in and through Jesus Christ. We know the freedom of knowing this truth. We know the ramifications of abusing this knowledge. And we know the faithfulness and justice of our King as He lovingly forgives us when we sin against Him, and the freedom found in this knowledge. We know. But not all people know.

Therefore, it is vital that we, as believers, purpose to love the one that is before and around us at any given time. It is imperative that we love the world in which we are shining His light. May we shine the same love that we have in and through Jesus Christ.

Knowledge and love must go hand in hand. If it does not, the Holy Spirit becomes limited within you.

Scripture:

> *However, not all possess this knowledge.*
> *But some, through former association with idols,*
> *eat food as really offered to an idol,*
> *and their conscience, being weak, is defiled.*
> *Food will not commend us to God.*
> *We are no worse off if we do not eat,*
> *and no better off if we do.*
> *1 Corinthians 8:7–8*

Knowledge. Paul understands our personal struggle in this area of what to eat and what to drink and what to do and what to wear and how to be a "good Christian girl." The challenge of how to be real; how to live in freedom; how to live without the bondage of man, law, and legalism — plus fakeness and judgment. The concept that knowledge is power is clear to Paul, and what is more powerful than the sweet knowledge of knowing Jesus Christ as your Lord and Savior? Here is a breath of renewal and strength, of identity and freedom, of newness and power — which is exactly what Jesus offers to us. It is exactly what Jesus desires to offer to the person beside you — wherever that may be. Therefore, Paul says, couple your knowledge of freedom with love.

Scripture:

> *But take care that this right of yours*
> *does not somehow become*
> *a stumbling block to the weak.*
> *For if anyone sees you who have knowledge*
> *eating in an idol's temple,*
> *will he not be encouraged,*
> *if his conscience is weak,*
> *to eat food offered to idols?*
> *And so, by your knowledge*
> *this weak person is destroyed,*
> *the brother for whom Christ died.*
> *1 Corinthians 8:9–11*

Love. Paul concludes God's truth through the life of Christ with his personal decision. What would happen if we took this truth, this knowledge that we know to be truth, and laid it before the Lord in prayer? What would happen if we said to God the Father that we desire to take this knowledge and mix it with our love for Jesus Christ? What would the outcome of our personal honesty before the Lord look like? Will you purpose to live out your love for Christ for the world in which you live?

May we not be pretentious. May we not be fake. May we not be resentful. For God loves a cheerful heart in all that we do, in all that we give, in all that we lovingly sacrifice for the greater purpose. Will you consider laying this chapter before the Throne in prayer today?

If you do accept this challenge, what, I wonder, will be your concluding decision? Paul stated his personal choice in verse 13. I encourage each of us not to model out of obligation but to live out of love — whatever that looks like for you and God.

Scripture:

> *Thus, sinning against your brothers*
> *and wounding their conscience when it is weak,*
> *you sin against Christ.*
> *Therefore, if food makes my brother stumble,*
> *I will never eat meat,*
> *lest I make my brother stumble.*
> *1 Corinthians 8:12–13*

Friend, your stumbling matters to God. Know that. It may be that you are one who struggles with stumbling over the decisions of others. If you are honest, you easily sway by the actions of another Christian. Or maybe Christians easily offend you by what they do not do.

Two types of Christians struggle with this. One is a Christian in a new place, a new season. Perhaps you are newly saved, and you are trying to figure out what is right and what is wrong. My advice for you is this:

learn from a stronger Christian without putting that person on a pedestal of "what I want to be when I grow up." This will only lead to judgment and disappointment. Is that fair to say? Yes, watch Christians that you respect. Learn from them, but do not emulate them. They are simply humans desiring to live for God through Christ Jesus. You do the same. Study to keep your eyes, your heart, your actions, and your decisions for God through Jesus Christ. Grow where you are. Grow as you are. This will allow the Holy Spirit to use you for the love of those around you. How beautiful is the life of a child of God!

The other Christian who battles this is the one who holds stones. May I be so bold? Perhaps this is the chapter that frees your hands from those "personal conviction stones." Figure out what your personal convictions are. As you focus on praying over your personal decisions for God through Christ Jesus, you will find yourself free from judging others. You will also notice that judgment from others no longer affects you. You will learn that knowledge and love bring freedom to your life and a deeper connection with others through the faithful leadership of the Holy Spirit.

There is such a sweet freedom when we know our decisions and keep them. Freedom in Christ deepens as we refrain from expecting others to abide by our convictions. What a powerful gift of proper judgment to offer to the One from whom and for whom all things exist.

Notes

1 Corinthians 9

*Am I not free? Am I not an apostle? Have I not seen Jesus our Lord?
Are not you my workmanship in the Lord? If to others I am not an apostle,
at least I am to you, for you are the seal of my apostleship in the Lord.*

*This is my defense to those who would examine me. Do we not have the
right to eat and drink? Do we not have the right to take along a believing wife,
as do the other apostles and the brothers of the Lord and Cephas? Or is it only
Barnabas and I who have no right to refrain from working for a living? Who
serves as a soldier at his own expense? Who plants a vineyard without eating
any of its fruit? Or who tends a flock without getting some of the milk?*

*Do I say these things on human authority? Does not the Law say the same?
For it is written in the Law of Moses, "You shall not muzzle an ox when it
treads out the grain." Is it for oxen that God is concerned? Does he not
certainly speak for our sake? It was written for our sake, because the plowman
should plow in hope and the thresher thresh in hope of sharing in the crop. If we
have sown spiritual things among you, is it too much if we reap material things
from you? If others share this rightful claim on you, do not we even more?*

*Nevertheless, we have not made use of this right, but we endure anything
rather than put an obstacle in the way of the gospel of Christ. Do you not
know that those who are employed in the temple service get their food from
the temple, and those who serve at the altar share in the sacrificial offerings?
In the same way, the Lord commanded that those who proclaim
the gospel should get their living by the gospel.*

But I have made no use of any of these rights, nor am I writing these things to secure any such provision. For I would rather die than have anyone deprive me of my ground for boasting. For if I preach the gospel, that gives me no ground for boasting. For necessity is laid upon me. Woe to me if I do not preach the gospel! For if I do this of my own will, I have a reward, but if not of my own will, I am still entrusted with a stewardship. What then is my reward? That in my preaching I may present the gospel free of charge, so as not to make full use of my right in the gospel.

For though I am free from all, I have made myself a servant to all, that I might win more of them. To the Jews I became as a Jew, in order to win Jews. To those under the law I became as one under the law (though not being myself under the law) that I might win those under the law. To those outside the law I became as one outside the law (not being outside the law of God but under the law of Christ) that I might win those outside the law. To the weak I became weak, that I might win the weak. I have become all things to all people, that by all means I might save some. I do it all for the sake of the gospel, that I may share with them in its blessings.

Do you not know that in a race all the runners run, but only one receives the prize? So run that you may obtain it. Every athlete exercises self-control in all things. They do it to receive a perishable wreath, but we an imperishable. So I do not run aimlessly; I do not box as one beating the air. But I discipline my body and keep it under control, lest after preaching to others I myself should be disqualified.

9

United in His Sight

I do it all for the sake of the gospel,
that I may share with them in its blessings.
1 Corinthians 9:23

D o you remember that rock-filled basket from Chapter 1? If you are anything like me, you already know what is lying around the corner, and your hands grip those stones tightly. These are the stones always with us, always on call. Will you consider, like we do with our cell phones at an elegant party, adding these to the basket?

Thank you.

Some are new to 1 Corinthians 9. Deep down you are wondering if you should gather a few pebbles in your purse just to be ready. Don't. Don't grab pebbles.

I remember driving home from a coffee shop Bible study on a Wednesday morning in the fall, and I heard the voice of the Lord press deeply on my heart. It took me a couple red lights to figure out the validity of what He was asking me to do. It just did not seem right. It took me another 20 minutes of sitting in my car before deciding to obey.

This memory carries weight to the truth of this chapter. It is a milestone of confirmation regarding the sound of the voice of God in my own life.

Paul says, *"For though I am free from all, I have made myself a servant to all, that I might win more of them."* (v. 19) I love this statement. Yet, its implication is difficult to personalize when judgment enters the room. This explains my opening request. Consider this your final call for a basket drop before Paul's opening statement pries your hand free.

Scripture:

Am I not free?
Am I not an apostle?
Have I not seen Jesus our Lord?
Are not you my workmanship in the Lord?
If to others I am not an apostle,
at least I am to you, for you are the seal
of my apostleship in the Lord.
This is my defense
to those who would examine me.
1 Corinthians 9:1–3

Paul's truth is his defense. He knew his standing as a member of society, in his position in the Lord, in his authority within the family of God. Furthermore, he had proof of his defense. Those very souls he led to the Lord and preached to are his defenders. To those who question him, he shrugs and points back to the truth, Jesus — and to those who know him.

Do you remember the stone of knowledge we dropped in the last chapter? The stone that we piously flick over to one who differs in our convictions or disagrees with our personal decisions. Those stones that prohibit grace and love to conquer and unify. Paul was dealing with these pebbles of knowledge as he traveled from church to church. Cross-examination from one person to the next must have been exhausting. Can you relate?

Questions regarding your choice of what you are eating and what you are drinking are endless, aren't they? Paul can relate.[55] What about judgment regarding your marital status? Ever get that? Why did you get married, why did you marry him, you should not be single, you should not get married...endless and slightly annoying, yes? Paul understands.[56] Paul and Barnabas were both single, and people had opinions that they did not need financial gain since they did not have a family to take care of. Kinda rude.[57]

Paul already covered his opinion on this matter of marriage and singlehood in the last chapter. He was not an advocate for marriage, so why should he get married? He had his heart set on other matters. For him, singlehood was correct and proper. However, being single comes with its costs. Literally. He was a working man. His work was not on the battlefield or tending to flocks, but he was defending the name of Christ and shepherding the children of God. That is work. Why shouldn't Paul get a paycheck for what he does?

There is much to glean from verses 4–22—quite a bit regarding the financial right of a gospel preacher. I do encourage you to read it and turn it over in prayer for the preacher who provides your study of the Word of God. However, with the depth of this chapter and our study on judgment, I would like to focus more on the remaining part of 1 Corinthians Chapter 9. Since you kindly left your stones at the door, I will assume you will not chuck one at my head for making this decision.

Again, thank you.

---

[55] 1 Corinthians 9:4
[56] 1 Corinthians 9:5
[57] 1 Corinthians 9:6–7

Scripture:

I do it all for the sake of the gospel,
that I may share with them in its blessings.
1 Corinthians 9:23

This is powerful. Its concept is revolutionary. Having practiced and penned years after Christ's resurrection, Paul shares with us what he learned from the day God blinded him on the road to Damascus[58] to this day as he recalls his personal encounters with different people throughout the years. Paul did not wake up from his blind encounter as the wise Apostle Paul. He earned it. He lived it. He learned how to be a man of God who desired to live as a light to the world around him. I am certain he had stories of success mingled with stories of failures. He had to learn how to behave before different people in different situations and in various cities. I am confident that these lessons had their challenges. Learning new things is difficult. Oh, but learning new things for the benefit of a lost soul is well worth the lessons that sit before us. In the end, Paul learned and formulated a plan of attack suitable for himself.

What would happen if I formulated a plan of attack that fit me and the world around me: my city, my church, my family, my grocery store, my coffee shops, my strangers? What if you developed a plan of attack that fits you and the world around you? The Light of the Lord would radiate throughout this world! Now, imagine if I followed my plan and you followed yours and neither of us judged one another's plan. There would be no place for the lost to hide. God could seek them out, speak truth in them, pour His love over them, and lead them to you or me. May we be the child of God — fit and ready — to meet all souls where they are so that we may lead them to Jesus.

Scripture:

To the Jews I became as a Jew,
in order to win Jews.

---

[58] Acts 9:3–9

To those under the law
I became as one under the law
(though not being myself under the law)
that I might win those under the law.
To those outside the law
I became as one outside the law
(not being outside the law of God
but under the law of Christ)
that I might win those outside the law.
To the weak I became weak,
that I might win the weak.
I have become all things to all people,
that by all means I might save some.
1 Corinthians 9:20–22

Paul looked at the world around him. As he viewed his outreach, he saw Jews who clung to the Old Testament, seeking the coming Messiah. He understood their duty to Abraham and met them where they were. Paul saw the law-abiders who craved a proper standing by the Roman law of the day. He watched as they obeyed the laws with perfection and without grumbling; Paul met them where they were. He guarded his words and personal thoughts of the government responsible for his stoning and imprisonments. He watched the Gentiles who walked as outsiders in a Jewish society. He witnessed their behaviors, noted their mentalities, yet held tight to his love for Jesus and met them where they were. Even the outcasts of each city were on Paul's radar. He purposed to see their need and to fill it with the Name that could heal. He invested in them to the point that he felt their pain. He became like the weak so that he could relate to and understand their individual hunger that only Jesus could satisfy. I can picture him sitting outside the city wall hearing the rebuke of others, feeling the hunger and sorrow that overtook their souls. He beheld those all around him for the sake of the gospel.

What do you see?

Using God's vision is vital. We will see this more in Chapter 12, but I think it would be grand to touch on the topic of the body of Christ for a moment. This chapter breeds judgment based on our perception of each other's actions. God gave a straightforward way to understand the function of the body of Christ by gifting us with a human body. There is much to compare between the two; therefore, there is much to learn and understand.

The purpose of the eye is to see; the intent of the ear is to hear. God created our hands to touch and our feet to step. None of these human parts have a mouth. None of these members has an opinion of what the other does. For this, we are ever so thankful. Imagine the fights that would go on if each body part could talk. Forget the insanity of taking a toddler to the grocery store; a disagreeable body would trump that exhaustion!

There are certain things that blind people from the truth of God's Word: religion, living under laws, binding themselves in careless living, battling with a weakness too hard to bear. This blinding is all around us, while we, the body of Christ, are setting our gaze on one another's actions and behaviors. No one has time for this gross display of judgment. Especially not the soul blinded by Satan, absently following the blind down the wide road to hell.

Our question ought to be this, "Which body part would be the best at placing itself under the law to win those under the law?" Ask this question as you read what Paul etched into this passage. Who? Who has God called and equipped to reach out to the weak? Who has God asked to speak truth to the Jew? To whom has God whispered a request? This is the question at hand. The answer, being simple, is you. And that is the only answer you need to focus on.

If God is asking you to be the eye, then see. If the ear, then hear. If the lungs, breathe. If the baby toe, balance. If the buttocks, sit. If the shoulder, carry. If the mouth, speak. If the elbow, be flexible. If the knee, oh sweet friend, pray. Learn from the human body and participate in the body of Christ. Do not worry about law-abiders. Do not worry about your flesh. Set your eyes on the One who rescued you and fight to rescue another.

No room for condemnation. No room for self-regression. This is not about you. Get over you. This is about Jesus.

Remember this: We started our study learning and knowing who we are in Jesus Christ. We first became sure of our person, then we saw our vitality in building the temple of God. Remember who you are and how you build. In this truth, we can see the power of this chapter. Who are you? You are the daughter of God! What is your purpose? To build the temple of Christ! How do you do it? You listen to the voice of God whispered upon your heart, and then you obey. And you begin this process today.

Scripture:

> *I do it all for the sake of the gospel,*
> *that I may share with them in its blessings.*
> 1 Corinthians 9:23

Such personal pronouns scripted in this verse! Everything Paul had said about *being all for all men* is his personal quest. His purpose being the benefits that he knows will wash over the soul before him. How devoted he is in awareness and intentionality! Whoever is in his viewpoint is the drive behind his next step. Paul remains surefooted in his salvation: armored with the shield of faith, protected by the helmet of salvation, and holding firm to the sword of truth as the gospel of peace directs his every step.

Yet in his armor, he presents himself in his humanity. Clad in Christ's righteousness, he becomes relatable to his audience. Paul identifies with Christ as he identifies with the truth of the soul in need of Jesus Christ.

This. This is his plan of attack. He came to the realization that Christianity begins with his relationship with God through Jesus Christ, then grew into a seed planted in God's written Word. A seed watered by the love of Jesus Christ and beautified by the breath of the Holy Spirit. And in the end, he concluded that the fruit of his seed has nothing to do with him but all to do with one more soul. Overall, he learned that in

Jesus there is now no condemnation.[59] Not on him or from him, not on others or from others. For the space is now filled with eyes set on eternity.

Here lies the caution tape. If temptation rises within you as spoken of in James 1:13–14, then redirect the situation. Let's say a friend asks you to meet her at the mall. She needs time with you, desperately. You want to be there for her, but your credit card is nearing a dangerous peak. You have been walking a tight path with financial expert Dave Ramsey trying your best to fix this situation. You smile at your friend, who is earnest in spending healing time with you, and offer an afternoon at a coffee shop instead of the mall. Purchasing a $4.69 latte is much wiser than window shopping at your favorite traps at the mall.

Situational wisdom applies to any area of temptation. You know you. More so, God knows you. Therefore, He will not ask you to stop by the wine shop on your way home when a bottle of wine is too easy to consume. The Holy Spirit will not ask you to run into an ice cream parlor, a bakery, or a pizzeria if your battle is with food. Drinking, smoking, movies, music, books, downtown, the skate shop, whatever it is that wakes up that raging battle within your flesh is not the call God will place in your life at this time. He knows you. He loves you. And He is fighting for your freedom from that chain.

We are part of a functional body that can cover one another. Our temptations differ. This is the greatest truth about the body. There are thousands of body parts that unite to function. When the foot cannot scratch an itch, our fingers can. When our shoulders cannot smell danger, our noses can. There is no jealousy from the foot or the shoulder but relief that a capable body part diverted the situation. No tension. No comparison. Simply unified agreement and extreme appreciation for each unique ability.

Scripture:

> *Do you not know*
> *that in a race all the runners run,*

---

[59] Romans 8:1

but only one receives the prize?
So run that you may obtain it.
Every athlete exercises self-control in all things.
They do it to receive a perishable wreath,
but we an imperishable.
So I do not run aimlessly;
I do not box as one beating the air.

But I discipline my body
and keep it under control,
lest after preaching to others
I myself should be disqualified.
1 Corinthians 9:24–27

Sweet Sister, if there is one truth that I implore you to grasp in this whole book, it is this: It is all about Jesus! Everything we say is about Jesus. All that we do is about Jesus. The way we dress is about Jesus. The speech that spills from our lips is about Jesus. Our consumption is about Jesus. Our worship is about Jesus. If the Spirit is whispering to your heart in one of these areas, listen. Perhaps He is desiring your words to be all about Jesus, or your actions, your dress, your everything. Growth happens in each of us in different seasons of life. Your goal is to be able to say with all your heart, "All that I do, I do for Jesus." Sister, stand proud in your individual ability to shine His light in the person you are today. God desires to use you as you are and where you are.

Grasp the depth of this simple truth! Once I understood this, I became free to become all things to all people. There is freedom in this understanding. No longer am I bound by your opinion of my behavior. For in that binding, I was not free to truly listen to the leading of the Savior. I was too worried about what you would think. You see, I knew what you were thinking, because I was thinking the same about our sister who made a choice with which I certainly did not agree.

Who am I to not agree with her decision? Furthermore, who am I to disagree with your decision? I do not know what the Lord just whispered in your heart. I do not know what part of your past the Lord desires to use for that lady sitting across from you at Applebee's. I have no idea what she needs from the Lord and from the Lord pouring out through you. I am not a guest at that table. My perception does not matter. It is all about Jesus. Do you see?

If Christ can enter the form of humanity to meet humanity where it is, then why can't we? Pharisees most certainly judged Jesus for eating with sinners. Why do we think that we will not be? Jesus did not care. Why should we?

If you are still grasping at that stone, may I direct your eyes to the classic memory verse found at the end of this chapter? In the light of our truth, read those words anew. "But I discipline my body and keep it under control, lest after preaching to others I myself should be disqualified." (v. 27) The premise of this chapter is about Jesus Christ. See that in its rooted truth. It's Jesus! And Christian Friend, it is personal. It is personal between you and Jesus, and it is personal between her and Jesus. Oh, that we will keep our eyes on Jesus and be willing for Him to use us as the human conduit for her salvation!

Do you remember my memory of driving home from a coffee shop one Wednesday morning in the fall? A whisper crossed my heart, and I laughed. It spoke a little louder, and I flicked a stone at the Spirit. My hands gripped the wheel as the pressing got louder and clearer. I veered my car from the left turn lane that leads to home and continued straight on a street called Eagle. It was noon and the traffic was heavy. I was thankful for the traffic and for the time to think this over. I was still debating with God as I parked my car outside a wine shop that I had never been in. I sat in my car staring at the wine shop.

As I walked in the door, the owner of the store hung up the phone. She walked over to me as if she knew me and asked, "What do you know about submission? Sometimes, I just don't get it!" That quickly, I wanted to sit with God over coffee and laugh in awe of His ways. The owner of the store was a sister in Christ who just hung up the phone with another sister who was heartbroken over the repercussions of ill-displayed submission. I knew all about that. I wrote a book on it. I had just left a coffee shop Bible study discussing that exact topic. God wanted to use me to settle the hearts of two strangers yet sisters in Christ. In a wine shop. On a fall day. Just another ordinary day.

Going to a wine shop was not a normal stop for me. But I am slowly starting to see that it is in those simple, non-normal moments that God's compassion is abundantly magnified.[60] Each time we replace the fear of judgment with heeding to God's voice, one more soul gets the opportunity to hear the gospel message.

God will speak to each of us in diverse ways and in different seasons for His purpose. Our stories will be beautifully unique. And the more we learn to hear and listen to His voice, the more our stories are going to be endless. Here are stories that impacted my willingness to trust the voice of the Lord.

One time, I approached a single guy in a bookstore with a smile and a hello. Approaching single guys with a smile and a hello ended after I got married. It had been a couple of years; I was out of my game. But this man stood there, alone, and visibly hopeless. As I got closer, I noticed he was staring at Bibles in the religion section. "I don't know what your question is, but I know the answer is Jesus," spilled from my nervous smile. Starting up conversations with single guys may not be my normal, but it is God's. God touched that man's heart that day; I was just simply there. Often, this man crosses my heart. Often, I lay this man in prayer at the foot of the cross.

One time, the Lord asked me to approach a stranger after a church event and to call her Linda. Not knowing her face or name, I confidently proclaimed a heartfelt, "Hey, Linda!" This stranger looked at me with tears in her eyes and said, "I needed to know that someone knew who I was." I had never seen this woman before. Confidently calling women by name may not be my comfort zone, but it is God's. Such a small, nerve-wracking moment in my life touched the heart of this woman in a way God knew she needed at that very moment.

---

[60] Matthew 18:12

One time, I learned about a TV show called, Dr. Who. A girl sitting before me in a cell phone store talked eagerly for about an hour all about her infatuation with this show. I had nothing to add to the conversation, for I still have little to no clue as to who Dr. Who may be. However, once she trickled her excitement to a close, she thanked me for just listening to her. When she thanked me for simply listening to her talk about a TV show, God nudged my heart. When this girl said to me that it was my turn to talk and hers to listen, I knew what God was nudging. I may not enjoy long, television show conversations, but God does. For in those long moments of listening, someone feels like their words matter. And they do. They matter to Jesus.

Then there was the first time. I was 16 years old and flew from Las Vegas to New York by myself. I was sitting in the middle seat. Doing what I do when I got scared, I pulled out my Bible and buried myself in the comforts of my favorite words. Between me and the window, sat a man named Bart. Bart raised his glass of whiskey at me with a kind smile and nod of acknowledgment. I did not know Bart, nor did I know Jack. But God did. This man asked me questions throughout our flight together. And I answered each one. Some of his answers I could answer out of my love and knowledge of the Scripture. Some of his questions were answered with statements bigger than mine. You see, as soon as Bart asked a question, an answer rang within me that made sense, so I said it aloud to a stranger as a sixteen-year-old. Jesus was the topic of conversation throughout this flight. One day, I will see Bart again because God met him where he was through the innocence of a sixteen-year-old girl.

Each of these moments was a one-time snapshot in my life. I grew in my willingness to trust the Lord's voice without changing my habits or my opinions or altering my personal convictions. Because none of these moments was about me. They were not about wine or single men or TV shows or calling strangers by their name or whiskey. These moments were about individual people that matter to Jesus.

There is normalcy in our daily way of life that repeats itself for most days of our lives. We like our normal everyday life and our personal standards. We are confident of our convictions. But we also need to like the presence of the Holy Spirit and be confident in His power in us when He speaks. We can be sure that when He asks us to do something outside of our normal way of life, He is going with us, and His plan will prove faithful.

Once we understand that we can be all things for all men while keeping our qualification as His daughter, then our individual plans of attack will become bigger than our ill-informed habit of stone throwing.

How easy it is to roll our eyes, point our fingers, throw our stones, and ignore the person before us. But I am telling you right now, it is just as easy to set our eyes, open our hands, drop our stones, and see the world before us. It is a constant choice that only we can make. How I pray we will make a compassionate choice!

One time, God used Christ as He stepped out of His normal way of life to share with us the gift of salvation.

Sometimes, God will use us as we step out of our normal way of life for the light of Jesus Christ to radiate in the life of another.

Sometimes, we...

> "... do it all for the sake of the gospel,
> that (we) may share with them in its blessings."
> 1 Corinthians 9:23

Notes

1 Corinthians 10

For I do not want you to be unaware, brothers, that our fathers were all under the cloud, and all passed through the sea, and all were baptized into Moses in the cloud and in the sea, and all ate the same spiritual food, and all drank the same spiritual drink. For they drank from the spiritual Rock that followed them, and the Rock was Christ. Nevertheless, with most of them God was not pleased, for they were overthrown in the wilderness.

Now these things took place as examples for us, that we might not desire evil as they did. Do not be idolaters as some of them were; as it is written, "The people sat down to eat and drink and rose up to play." We must not indulge in sexual immorality as some of them did, and twenty-three thousand fell in a single day. We must not put Christ to the test, as some of them did and were destroyed by serpents, nor grumble, as some of them did and were destroyed by the Destroyer.

Now these things happened to them as an example, but they were written down for our instruction, on whom the end of the ages has come. Therefore let anyone who thinks that he stands take heed lest he fall. No temptation has overtaken you that is not common to man. God is faithful, and he will not let you be tempted beyond your ability, but with the temptation he will also provide the way of escape, that you may be able to endure it.

Therefore, my beloved, flee from idolatry. I speak as to sensible people; judge for yourselves what I say. The cup of blessing that we bless, is it not a participation in the blood of Christ? The bread that we break, is it not a participation in the body of Christ? Because there is one bread, we who are many are one body, for we all partake of the one bread. Consider the people of Israel: are not those who eat the sacrifices participants in the altar? What do I imply then?

That food offered to idols is anything, or that an idol is anything? No, I imply that what pagans sacrifice they offer to demons and not to God. I do not want you to be participants with demons. You cannot drink the cup of the Lord and the cup of demons. You cannot partake of the table of the Lord and the table of demons. Shall we provoke the Lord to jealousy? Are we stronger than he?

"All things are lawful," but not all things are helpful. "All things are lawful," but not all things build up. Let no one seek his own good, but the good of his neighbor. Eat whatever is sold in the meat market without raising any question on the ground of conscience. For "the earth is the Lord's, and the fullness thereof." If one of the unbelievers invites you to dinner and you are disposed to go, eat whatever is set before you without raising any question on the ground of conscience. But if someone says to you, "This has been offered in sacrifice," then do not eat it, for the sake of the one who informed you, and for the sake of conscience — I do not mean your conscience, but his. For why should my liberty be determined by someone else's conscience? If I partake with thankfulness, why am I denounced because of that for which I give thanks?

So, whether you eat or drink, or whatever you do, do all to the glory of God. Give no offense to Jews or to Greeks or to the church of God, just as I try to please everyone in everything I do, not seeking my own advantage, but that of many, that they may be saved.

10

United in Jesus

Do not be idolaters as some of them were; as it is written,
"The people sat down to eat and drink and rose up to play."
Therefore, my beloved, flee from idolatry.
1 Corinthians 10:7, 14

In my day-to-day existence, there are moments that I do this little thing within my little self. A thought will pop into my head, and then as quickly as a jackrabbit flees the tight embrace of an over-eager hugger, I take that little thought and invite it in as my identity. These lies soar deep into my soul and overwhelm my ability to see anything good about myself. This day-to-day event can whip from my brain to my baby toe in a nanosecond. These thoughts are not kind thoughts. Old-school moms would wash these out with soap if their ears ever heard them. These lies just fly out of nowhere—frequently. Yet, I put up with it. My husband, not so much. He does not like the expression that crosses my face before the internal dialogue takes over. He does not appreciate my being so mean to his bride.

I had two choices to make. One, bully myself and believe what I say. Two, write down the words that my husband says to me, repeat them aloud and believe his words over mine when I begin to bully myself.

I picked option two.

I found out option two was a little easier than option one. Although my habitual self-bullying was a natural reaction, quoting Don louder than my thoughts was fulfilling. His words built me up. His words of truth began to ring louder than my ingrained lies.

Moments in the day-to-day overtook some of the Israelites. For some it was idolatry,[61] for others it was sexual immorality,[62] for some it was putting Christ to the test,[63] and for others it was grumbling.[64] I wonder what these actions looked like, how deeply these acts and temptations and words were rooted. I wonder how a struggling Israelite lived day by day with these burrowing roots.

Perhaps we do not need to wonder; maybe we know all too well. If we were to compare our mental snapshot of the Israelites with our over-active reality of today, we could easily see the similarities between the Israelites and New Testament believers. However, something separates their reality from ours.

Paul says, "Judge for yourself what I am saying about this matter." I say that we accept that challenge with our sharpened understanding of living without the condemnation of stone throwing judgment.

Scripture:

> *For I do not want you to be unaware, brothers,*
> *that our fathers were all under the cloud,*
> *and all passed through the sea,*
> *and all were baptized into Moses*
> *in the cloud and in the sea,*
> *and all ate the same spiritual food,*

---

[61] Exodus 32:1–6
[62] Numbers 25:1–9
[63] Numbers 21:4–9; John 3:14–15
[64] Exodus 15:24, 16:2, 17:3

> *and all drank the same spiritual drink.*
> *For they drank from the spiritual Rock*
> *that followed them,*
> *and the Rock was Christ.*
> *1 Corinthians 10:1–4*

Can we see our similarities to the Israelites in this passage? It is rather stunning. It shocked me. I do not remember these details so clearly expressed. Then again, I avoided reading 1 Corinthians with burning passion. Perhaps that is why these four verses are eye-opening to me today.

God's people in the Old Testament were all under the cloud of God, they experienced the symbolism of baptism both in the cloud and in the sea, they ate the same food provided by God in remembrance of God's hand over them, and they drank of the same water from the same Rock which is Christ.

In comparison, God's people in the New Testament were all under the providential hand of God—baptized in the Spirit and in the water. They ate the same bread in remembrance of God's gift of Salvation over them, and they drank of the wine that was the representation of Jesus Christ crucified and risen again.

The details of the similarities between the Old and New Testament believers overwhelm our modern-day mentality of casting judgment on our family members of long ago.

We are no different. We are the same in humanity and in action and in Christ. One thing, however, separates our reality from theirs.

While present with Moses on the mountain,[65] God heard the hearts, the words, and the actions of His people down in the valley. He heard His people complain about their situations—the slur of words that shot out like a cannon full of contempt, complaint, and dissatisfaction. He

---

[65] Exodus 32:18

133

watched their spiritual leader, Aaron, settle their complaints by offering a golden solution.

Further still, He saw the actions of sexual immorality. His children tested His presence up against an idol. They were willing to put up with these actions, carrying on for hours and hours. They prepared food and shared it with one another. They provided drinks to bond their celebration together. They partook in actions that are unbecoming of a righteous people. How God's heart broke over the thoughts and words and actions of his chosen people.

All the while, Moses was with God as God listened and witnessed the behavior of His people. Moses recorded his response for us in Exodus 32:11–33. His first reaction was to comfort the heart of God. Oh, to be that friend to God! He consoled God's heartbreak and settled his anger. Moses did this by reminding God of His promise to his friends: Abraham, Isaac, and Jacob. He reminded God of His promise to himself and to His chosen people. He, also, set God's eyes on the unsaved nations around them by asking God, *what evil will they say about you, the God of the Israelites?* Yes, Moses was a friend to God!

His next reaction was to go down the mountain. He met the Israelites where they were: wined, dined and gathered in disgrace around a golden image. Yes, Moses was a leader to the people. We may say he overreacted, that his anger blew out of proportion. But when I put myself in his reality with God's predicted power sitting before him, seeing the mighty glory of the One and Only True and Living God, and seeing his brother and his flock behaving with such emptiness as to who God is, I see Moses as a leader among leaders.

The result of his anger portrayed the sovereignty of God. Aaron's position as priest God graciously spared. The lives of all the Levites, who refused to participate in the debauchery, God rightfully protected. Those who swore love to God one day and paraded themselves before an idol the next were all taken.

It is imperative that we see the actions of our forefathers not in judgment but in example. These were humans living day by day in their normal reality. We tend to picture them as flannel graph characters from Sunday School classes from back in the day, but they were just like you and me. They were women, wives, mothers who spent their days preparing food, tending to their families, worshipping God Almighty in the protection of His hand. But they gave place to their thoughts letting them seep within and eventually shoot out of a cannon with full fury.

Nothing with God has changed. He is always and forever, the beginning and the end. He created all things, and He created all things for Himself. He sacrificed His Son out of His great love for all mankind. He loves all of us, equally. He was there yesterday, and He is here today.

God sees the similarities between you and me and the Israelite people. He sees and He knows. In His understanding, He provided a way out of this cyclical self-depredation. It is this way out that stands as the difference between them and us.

Scripture:

> *No temptation has overtaken you*
> *that is not common to man.*
> *God is faithful,*
> *and he will not let you be tempted*
> *beyond your ability,*
> *but with the temptation*
> *he will also provide the way of escape,*
> *that you may be able to endure it.*
> *Therefore, my beloved, flee from idolatry.*
> *I speak as to sensible people;*
> *judge for yourselves what I say.*
> *1 Corinthians 10:13–15*

The Israelites were in a new transition as a nation. They were learning to live in freedom after existing as slaves for four hundred years.[66] They

---

[66] Exodus 15:13; Acts 7:6

received everything they needed to survive in their newfound freedom. They had God (the cloud), they had the Spirit (the fire), and they had Christ (the rock). They had physical leaders in Moses and Aaron; they had daily food and a constant supply of water. Furthermore, they had one another.

The Corinthians were in a new transition as a body post Christ's earthly resurrection. They, too, were learning how to live in the freedom of Christ after living under the Roman Law for about two hundred years. They had everything they needed in God, in the Spirit, and in Christ Jesus. They had physical leaders in Peter (Cephas) and Paul. They had two daily provisions as a reminder of what they have in Christ: bread and wine. Furthermore, they had one another.

Herein lies the beautiful contrast. Such hope overwhelms at the beautiful simplicity that remains. What smile overtakes my heart as I sit in this contrasted jewel of truth! Moses and Aaron led the Israelites out of a captivity into a promised future, but they never saw their reward.[67] Peter and Paul led the followers of Jesus out of the old covenant into an eternal future, and they daily received their reward.

The difference lies in the person of Jesus Christ.

Christ was present with the Israelites.[68] He was the Rock that sustained their water supply. But they never *knew* Jesus Christ. Jesus was present with the disciples. He walked with them daily, teaching them the mysteries of God, showing them the power of the Holy Spirit, and proclaiming His position in the Godhead.

Peter was the first disciple to recognize that Jesus was the Christ the Son of God.[69] Paul realized who Jesus was after he saw the resurrected Christ.[70] Neither of these men got over their relationship with Him. Jesus

---

[67] Deuteronomy 32:48–52
[68] 1 Corinthians 10:4; Exodus 17:6; Numbers 20:7–13
[69] Matthew 16:13–20
[70] 1 Corinthians 15:8 (4–11)

was their Friend; Christ was their Savior. Nothing could shake that knowledge, minimize that experience, or decrease that love.

You and I are in a new challenge as believers. We are learning to live in the freedom of judgment. We have everything we need to accept and excel in this challenge. We have the love of God over us,[71] the love of Jesus under us,[72] and the Holy Spirit alive within us.[73] We have physical leaders at our local churches. We have the same two daily provisions set as a reminder of what we have in Christ: bread and wine. Furthermore, we have one another.

How important it is to look back at our forefathers with the desire to learn from them, not to judge them. What they faced, we face. What they felt, we feel. Their struggles and their temptations are no different than our struggles and temptations. Life is common.[74] Humanity is cyclical in behavior. Temptations are an ever-present reality.

But God. God is faithful, and He will not suffer us to be overcome with the common temptations of mankind. This is the beauty and the power of Jesus Christ.

Too often, we focus so much on not sinning that we forget to love Jesus. If sin is a constant struggle for you, then look back at the Israelites and learn from them. *"Nevertheless, with most of them God was not pleased, for they were overthrown in the wilderness."* (v.5) They did not lose their position in God, but they lost out on their reward in the Promised Land. Their hang-ups? Lust (Num. 11:4, 33–34), idolatry (Ex.32:6), sexual sin (Num. 25:1–18), testing God (Num. 21:6) and complaining (Num. 14, 16).

Lust. Complaining. My hand is raised. And when I walk through my day with that hand raised, I always feel like a failure. I cannot seem to rise higher than my hand. Did the Israelites struggle with always seeing

---

[71] Psalm 119:41–43
[72] Psalm 118:22; Acts 4:11–12
[73] Ephesians 4:30; Romans 5:5; 1 Corinthians 6:19
[74] 1 Corinthians 10:13

themselves with their hands raised? I wonder if they always saw themselves as a slave. Did this mentality explain the habits of their past? I don't know; I simply wonder.

Here we see the first followers of Jesus Christ put down their hands. Peter had a quick tongue, James and John had anger management issues, and Paul persecuted the Church. These behaviors were their reputations for too long. People that knew them knew their behaviors. After Jesus Christ rose from death and the grave, they refused to claim their sin as an identity any longer. They knew Jesus!

I wish someone had told me to read 1 Corinthians through the love of Jesus rather than with the fear of sin. What a game changer! Temptation is going to happen[75] because we are human. Satan has an insatiable hatred toward us. Our eyes are forever seeing "delightful" things, and our flesh is always hungry for more. It is as if we are set up for failure courtesy of Lucifer and Eve. But we know Jesus.

Oh, Friend. Forget Heads Up, Seven Up. Jesus put the raised hand of our past down and stands us up beside Him in His light, in His way, for His glory and full of His love. No longer are we under the law of sin (Satan) and death (Eve): We are alive through Christ Jesus our Lord! So, whether you eat or drink, or whatever you do, do everything for the glory of God. You are free to live your life loved and in love with your Lord Jesus Christ.

It is in this power and knowledge of Christ Jesus that we heed to Paul's exhortation regarding idolatry. Proper judgment deepens understanding within our own lives. I pray that we will demonstrate proper judgment in this matter of idolatry. I pray our fitting judgment will deepen our understanding of those in the greater family of God.

---

[75] 1 Corinthians 10:13; 1 Peter 5:8; 1 John 2:15–17; James 1:13–16

Scripture:

> *Therefore, my beloved, flee from idolatry.*
> *I speak as to sensible people;*
> *judge for yourselves what I say.*
> *1 Corinthians 10:14–15*

First, we must understand what idolatry is. Idolatry is bigger than putting Fox News before reading Psalm 15. It is bigger than putting the Super Bowl before Sunday evening service. And it is bigger than putting the cravings of your flesh before the desires of the Spirit. These three examples speak to us in the comforts of our American pews. We try to bring an understanding of idolatry to our life circumstances. But, my friend, these are choices we make; they are not idolatry.

Idolatry is using gold, silver, and precious stones to build up a nonliving entity. This is exactly what the Israelite nation was guilty of doing simultaneously to the scribing of the Ten Commandments. And this is what the residents of Corinth were accustomed to doing in the temples located throughout their city. Idolatry is using precious metals for the glorifying of a god in place of The God. This is idolatry.

Idolatry was a reality in the lives of these Corinthian believers. The struggle and the temptation were real. Let us not naturally condemn believers who also struggle with the *"temptation that is common to man."* (v.13) There are brothers and sisters throughout this world whom God saved out of idol-based worship. There are members of the body of Christ today raised in nations whose idols are their gods. To worship an idol is daily normalcy. Then Jesus meets them where they are. Jesus makes Himself known to them. Jesus Christ becomes their God. But their flesh and their nation and their habits and their normalcy are still present.

Oh, American Christians, may I speak directly to us for a moment? I pray that we will take the heart of this message to greater levels of understanding about the struggles of our family members around the world. May we use our understanding to pray for them, uplift them, guide them, and encourage them to faithfully build their lives upon the foundation of Jesus Christ. May we not judge their natural-man tendencies as they strive to use gold, silver, and precious jewels in a whole new way.

If you are looking for a specific example on properly judging an idolatrous situation, then you are in the right chapter of 1 Corinthians.

Scripture:

*If one of the unbelievers invites you to dinner
and you are disposed to go,
eat whatever is set before you
without raising any question
on the ground of conscience.
But if someone says to you,
"This has been offered in sacrifice,"
then do not eat it,
for the sake of the one who informed you,
and for the sake of conscience –
I do not mean your conscience, but his.
1 Corinthians 10:27–29a*

In Chapter 8, we learned not to judge others by what they eat. Food does not bring us closer to God. Nor does the absence of food bring us closer to God. We are to know our bodies, know our system, thank the Lord for providing, and then eat accordingly. Oh, and to not judge other believers for knowing their bodies, knowing their system, thanking the Lord, and eating.

In Chapter 9, we saw that our Christian status is bigger than us. Being a Christian is about being present where we are to the person before us that she might believe. It is about knowing that we are free from the chains of our past and of religion. Also, in our freedom, we are slaves to the salvation of another.

Here, we blend our freedom to eat with our vision for salvation while keeping our devotion to the Savior.

The scene is set before you. The invitation to dine at an associate's house has arrived. You are not entirely thrilled to attend, for you know they are partakers in the city's natural function. This is not going to be a fun night—you just know it. But a friend invited you, and you have nothing on your calendar to prohibit your attending. Your hair is even freshly washed.

To your surprise, it is a pleasant evening. The ambience well thought out, the attendees are kind, and the food looks and smells divine. Internally, you are belittling yourself for judging the event before giving it a chance. "Why do I do that?" you ask yourself. Sighing inside, you smile at those nearest you.

They serve the main dish, at last. It tastes as good as it looks. *Thank you, Lord.*

The host stands, taps his knife to his glass, and offers a toast of thanks to the god to which this meat had been offered. He shares his belief in and adoration to this god. And he is thrilled at the price he paid for it earlier that day.

Well. Hmph.

The truth is it is just food. Furthermore, it is food that you thanked the Lord for, making it worthy of consumption. But the deeper truth is, it is no longer about what is on the table, nor is it about you. This is about devotion to the Lord and Savior as the One and Only true God.

Again, remember Paul is setting this scene for the early Corinthian believers dwelling in a city known for its filthy idolatry. This scene was a common occurrence. Devotion to the "New Jesus" was not common. There was a choice to make. And that choice was so much bigger than them. The choice was Jesus.

The choice is always Jesus. What a shame to choose selfish gain over devotion to the Lord Jesus. If you know the choice to partake will cause your audience to question your devotion to Christ Jesus as your Savior, then do not partake at that very moment.

Eat and drink in the love of Jesus; the natural reaction (per circumstance) will flow out of you on behalf of the salvation of another.[76] Apply His devotion to us in such minimal matters all the while not judging others for partaking in options for the goal of the salvation of another.

Oh, yes, it is a fine line. Let me tell you! Yes, the temptation to judge with condemnation is common to man, but God is faithful, and He has made a way to escape. I pray we will keep our devotion on our unified path, for in doing so, stones of judgment will easily slip through our fingertips freeing our hands to build one another up.

Scripture:

> *So, whether you eat or drink,*
> *or whatever you do,*
> *do all to the glory of God.*
> *Give no offense to Jews or to Greeks*
> *or to the church of God,*
> *...that they may be saved.*
> *1 Corinthians 10:31–33*

While we practice an understanding of those tempted to the ways of idol worship, I pray you and I are sensitive to the temptations of others. Let us not perceive their temptation as a greater pit than our own. [77] No good will come of this. Certainly, no salvation will, either.

Rather, look to the examples laid out before us in this chapter and in Exodus 32. See the common temptations felt throughout the ages. May we not use this commonality as an expression of freedom but as an encouragement to overcome.

---

[76] 1 Corinthians 10:31–33; Mark 10:45
[77] Colossians 3:1–15

Stand in Truth

Just as I shared my struggle of begrudging myself to the point of shame and heartache, the Israelites struggled with their words of complaint to the point of snake attacks.[78] The battle is real.

But the way out is so much sweeter and easier to attain.

My husband opened the door for me to learn this truth. He taught me how to hear his truth and to speak it over my perceived lies. God the Father speaks truth over you. It is up to you to hear His truth and to speak it louder than your internal dialogue.

Whether your temptation be of lust, idolatry, sexual sin, testing God, or complaining, there is truth sprinkled throughout the written Word of God. Study the Scriptures. Find the truth that stirs your heart to life. Believe His truth over the lies of temptation. Memorize His love. And proclaim it every time the smoke of temptation attempts to form around you.

And, Friend, take advantage of having one another in your lives. God has endless reasons why He designed His people to unite as a family. This is one of the most beautiful aspects of being in His family (personal opinion)! We are to be there for one another. Furthermore, we *need* to be there for one another.

Temptation is common to mankind. This is not our excuse but our truth. If we fail to look at our individual temptation as common, and if we refuse to tell a trusted friend, then we are choosing to turn our battle over to the dark side of loneliness. To conquer a battle within ourselves is often a cyclical loss.

The very week I was working on this chapter, I was battling my internal dialogue like I have not in years. It sideswiped me—took my breath away. I found myself on my closet floor weeping with disdain of the mirror's image. I felt broken.

---

[78] Numbers 21:4–9; John 3:14–15

Then I talked with three friends. I told them about my Sunday morning just three days prior to our coffee date. I fought tears as I retold my embarrassing angst. And then I listened. I listened to the words that fed my soul.

Here's the thing. Their words were not of pity or condemnation or empty words that would fill my head for the moment but not for my war. They understood. They knew my battle because they had fought the same battle.

There is, Sweet Sister, no temptation that is not common to mankind. If we do not share our truths with one another, then we cannot hold one another up. Furthermore, we cannot conclude such difficult conversations with truly needful medicinal laughter!

Throughout time, God has given His people everything we need to survive this journey of life. We have God and His Word. We have His Son and His daughters. We have the presence and the promise of the Holy Spirit.

Quoting God louder than your temptation will be fulfilling. His words will build you up. His words of truth will ring louder than all ingrained lies. For His Truth is the way of escape.

Notes

Jaclyn Palmer

1 Corinthians 11

Be imitators of me, as I am of Christ.

Now I commend you because you remember me in everything and maintain the traditions even as I delivered them to you. But I want you to understand that the head of every man is Christ, the head of a wife is her husband, and the head of Christ is God. Every man who prays or prophesies with his head covered dishonors his head, but every wife who prays or prophesies with her head uncovered dishonors her head, since it is the same as if her head were shaven. For if a wife will not cover her head, then she should cut her hair short. But since it is disgraceful for a wife to cut off her hair or shave her head, let her cover her head. For a man ought not to cover his head, since he is the image and glory of God, but woman is the glory of man. For man was not made from woman, but woman from man. Neither was man created for woman, but woman for man. That is why a wife ought to have a symbol of authority on her head, because of the angels. Nevertheless, in the Lord woman is not independent of man nor man of woman; for as woman was made from man, so man is now born of woman. And all things are from God. Judge for yourselves: is it proper for a wife to pray to God with her head uncovered? Does not nature itself teach you that if a man wears long hair it is a disgrace for him, but if a woman has long hair, it is her glory? For her hair is given to her for a covering. If anyone is inclined to be contentious, we have no such practice, nor do the churches of God.

But in the following instructions I do not commend you, because when you come together it is not for the better but for the worse. For, in the first place, when you come together as a church, I hear that there are divisions among you. And I believe it in part, for there must be factions among you in order that those who are genuine among you may be recognized. When you come together, it is not the Lord's supper that you eat. For in eating, each one goes ahead with his own meal. One goes hungry, another gets drunk. What!

Do you not have houses to eat and drink in? Or do you despise the church of God and humiliate those who have nothing? What shall I say to you? Shall I commend you in this? No, I will not.

For I received from the Lord what I also delivered to you, that the Lord Jesus on the night when he was betrayed took bread, and when he had given thanks, he broke it, and said, "This is my body, which is for you. Do this in remembrance of me." In the same way also he took the cup, after supper, saying, "This cup is the new covenant in my blood. Do this, as often as you drink it, in remembrance of me." For as often as you eat this bread and drink the cup, you proclaim the Lord's death until he comes.

Whoever, therefore, eats the bread or drinks the cup of the Lord in an unworthy manner will be guilty concerning the body and blood of the Lord. Let a person examine himself, then, and so eat of the bread and drink of the cup. For anyone who eats and drinks without discerning the body eats and drinks judgment on himself. That is why many of you are weak and ill, and some have died. But if we judged ourselves truly, we would not be judged. But when we are judged by the Lord, we are disciplined so that we may not be condemned along with the world.

So then, my brothers, when you come together to eat, wait for one another — if anyone is hungry, let him eat at home — so that when you come together it will not be for judgment. About the other things I will give directions when I come.

11

Love Jesus, Evidently

Judge for yourselves:
is it proper for a wife to pray to God
with her head uncovered?
Does not nature itself teach you
that if a man wears long hair
it is a disgrace for him,
but if a woman has long hair,
it is her glory?
1 Corinthians 11:13–15a

Oh, how my blood boils within my veins! Dramatic — perhaps. But let me tell you! This chapter has been a nemesis to my core for far too long. Such a rival that as I sat in Nancy Jane Salon in the spring of 2018 watching Kayla dutifully cut nine inches off my hair, this passage is what filled my head. Do not get me wrong, I love my salon appointments. I frequent them every seven to nine weeks — each time getting my hair colored, cut, and styled. The normal cut is for maintenance, you know, split ends and all. Not nine inches. Not losing my "New Testament glory." Certainly not battling Scripture in my head as my smile grew at my new reflection. Such a juxtaposition within my soul.

Why is this passage in the Bible? And why is this the segway Paul uses to divert our eyes from seeing the world around us with the eyes of God to seeing the body of Christ with the love of God? Why hair? Why now?

Scripture:

> *Be imitators of me,*
> *as I am of Christ.*
> *Now I commend you*
> *because you remember me in everything*
> *and maintain the traditions*
> *even as I delivered them to you.*
> *But I want you to understand...*
> *1 Corinthians 11:1–3a*

Like his exhortations in Thessalonians[79] and Romans,[80] Paul exhorts the Corinthians in their upholding of the "traditions" of the Faith: Salvation by Christ alone, righteousness washed over them by the Holy Spirit, and eternal life given to them by the Heavenly Father. Pursue, he says, fight and take hold of these more than anything else.

More often than not, when we hear the word tradition in Scripture, we think of Old Testament laws. Here, Paul is defining the New Testament tradition as loving Jesus, evidently. May we wash those three words over these sixteen verses of hair chatter and call it good. Love Jesus, evidently. According to Paul, the Corinthian believers were doing well in their traditions. He commended them for remembering them and maintaining all they learned, but something was missing.

The image of Christ was missing. 1 Corinthians Chapter 10 spelled out the faults of idolatry. It opened our eyes to the danger of placing our heart before an image that took over the image of Christ in our life. Idolatry is

---

[79] 2 Thessalonians 2:15, 3:6
[80] Romans 6:17

a heart issue. It is bigger than sleeping in on Sunday morning. It is neglecting God from your life every day of the week. It is claiming Christ for salvation but ignoring Christ in your faith.

Then we see this topic of hair that seems to be perfectly out of place, and we wonder why? Why is Paul choosing our heads to transition our hearts to the next four chapters regarding the body of Christ?

God created us in the image of Christ. Our appearance matters. And — I believe — Paul chose to approach the topic the way he did because there is more to see than meets the eye. Oh, that we will see this passage with a new vision grounded on knowledge and understanding!

Scripture:

> *But I want you to understand*
> *that the head of every man is Christ,*
> *the head of a wife is her husband,*
> *and the head of Christ is God.*
> *Every man who prays or prophesies*
> *with his head covered dishonors his head,*
> *but every wife who prays or prophesies*
> *with her head uncovered*
> *dishonors her head,*
> *since it is the same as if her head were shaven.*
> *1 Corinthians 11:3–5*

Before getting into the discussion of hair measurements, let us talk submission. Because that is always the easier path to tread. You know, because we all love submission so much that we desire to create snow angels in the nearest rock garden. Don't. Don't make snow angels there.

Before flinging rocks at Paul, listen to his Biblical truth. *"The head of every man is Christ, the head of a wife is her husband, and the head of Christ is God."* If we untangle this sentence, we will see a positional chart starting with God as the head of Christ, Christ the head of every man, then a husband the head of his wife. May I ask you to see that Biblical truth as protection rather than inequality?

It begins with God. It always begins with God. God remains on His Throne, crowned in His deity. Always. He is the First and the Last, the Alpha and Omega. He is the Creator of the universe and the lover of our souls. He is God Almighty who craves to be our Father God. He is the great and everlasting I AM. Always and Forever. In His holiness, He desired relational connection with you and me despite our inherited humanity.

Enter Jesus Christ, the Son of God. Being equal with God, He chose to humble himself and took on the form of man, embraced a wooden cross, felt the sting of death, enclosed himself in separation from God above, and sang a song of Victory over it all. Jesus Christ, the Creator of the universe and the lover of our souls, chose you and me over His position of God. Sitting eternally on the right hand of the Throne of God, He chose submission to His Father so we, in our humanity, could have a relationship with God washed in Jesus' holiness.

Enter man, created in the image of the Father and the Son and the Holy Spirit, perfectly designed for God's glory. He was chosen to be an image bearer for the world around him. God created Adam whole but removed a piece, for man had a void without a woman.

Enter woman, created in the image of the Father and the Son and the Holy Spirit, perfectly designed for God's glory. She was chosen to be an image bearer for the world around her. God created Eve whole and for the fulfilling of the void within man. Man and woman, united as one, declare the completeness of God's design.

As man and as woman, we are to submit to Christ as Christ submitted to God, *For God is the head of Christ and Christ is the head of man.* It is a free choice to claim Christ for our salvation and to submit to Him in our faith.

As man and as woman, we have additional positions as husband and wife. Not all mankind lives in this realm, but for those of us who do, we need to be extra mindful of the positions listed in this passage: God, Christ, husband, wife. This position of submission introduces the gift of Communion for a reason, and we must understand it.

Living in a day where sexism is a rampant topic of conversation, I must declare this truth: Sexism matters to God. What matters to Him, however, is not that we stand for what we think but that we stand for the truth of who we are. We are women. We are wives. We need to stand as a woman created in the image of God. Also, we need to stand as a wife in submission to our husband as our husband stands in submission to Christ and Christ stands in submission to God. It's all or nothing. It is our image — the very image created in us to display to the world around us.

Scripture:

> *For if a wife will not cover her head,*
> *then she should cut her hair short.*
> *But since it is disgraceful for a wife*
> *to cut off her hair or shave her head,*
> *let her cover her head.*
> *For a man ought not to cover his head,*
> *since he is the image and glory of God,*
> *but woman is the glory of man.*
> *1 Corinthians 11:6–7*

And here we are, full circle to the cutting of the hair. May I just be real for a moment? I do not like using my moments as a writer to dig into the stories of my past, not when they have the full right to stay where they are. But at the recommendation of my husband, I will share the words spoken to me. My prayer is that my accounts will settle your heart, knowing that you are not alone in this realm of Christian judgment. I pray you will be able to leave those words in the past and press on in the new confidence of bearing the image of Jesus.

"Don't let her cut her hair. If you do, she will want to do everything rebellious." The words were spoken from a person of authority spoken to my soon-to-be husband.

"You are rebellious. One day you will understand." I asked if elderly women lose their glory when they get older and have short hair.

"You are a babe in Christ. One day you will mature and understand." I wore a ballcap considered inappropriate headwear by leadership.

Entering my adult years, I wanted to know what length achieved "full glory." Each time I asked, the accusation of being rebellious was the response. I just wanted to know where hair needed to measure on a ruler, you know, to be "full of glory." I never got my answer. Not by man, anyway.

As I sat there letting Kayla cut my hair (as short as that one time in college with the goal of getting this guy to break up with me), I was a fluttered disaster inside. Although I have always been confident and comfortable in my conversation with my God, I also knew Scripture. And the opinions that came with it. I wanted to know if anything was going to change in my walk with God. I wanted to know if my husband was going to think differently (even though this hairstyle was upon his suggestion. Spoiler alert: He loves it). I wanted to know if the Spirit of God was going to leave me. I wanted to know if I was going to lose the wisdom that I spent years asking the Lord for, just as He directed me to do. I wanted to know what was going to happen the morning after my haircut.

Do you know what happened? I learned the answer to my lifelong questions.

If I cut my hair, I will not desire all rebelliousness. When an elderly woman has short hair, she does not lose her glory. Her children rise up and call her blessed — but not because of her hair. The family of God holds her, protects her, cares for her, loves her. She teaches us how to love our husbands and raise our children and how to love our God. I do not think God would desire such a teacher of jewels to come from someone who has lost her glory through the natural progression of age.

I learned that a hat is a hat, and a haircut is a haircut. I learned that when our heart is in God and Christ is in our heart, our image will transform into his glory.[81] Regardless of the ballcap or the short haircut, my countenance claims my identity in Christ because it spills from His Spirit. I learned that our glory does not measure on a ruler, but that it measures in His love.

Today, my silly, little hair is still short, and I still love it! I continue to pray and speak His truth. My love for my husband and son is ever-present. And, above all, I still have the Spirit of the Lord reigning within me.

For you, who received judgment according to another's opinion, I am sorry. Please separate that gross display of twisted Scripture from the truth of this passage.

Here is some truth that can help heal your heart:

Did you know there was a plethora of prostitution in the city of Corinth? That the temples throughout the city allowed the act of prostitution to be on display? And that the image of a prostitute was a shaved head?

Remember to whom Paul is writing this passage. When we understand the culture around these people and the image of shame that separates a prostitute from a wife, this passage becomes less about us and our hair and our head coverings, and more about the Corinthian believers. Ponder this truth for a moment. The reason Paul says to the Corinthian believers that it is shameful for a woman to cut her hair or to shave her head is because prostitution proudly paraded itself within their culture. Paul is saying, do not look like the prostitute of the city whose very act brings attention to the idolatrous temples of the city.

In short, Paul was detailing a plea to bear the image of Christ rather than the image of idolatrous prostitution. That's fair. As far as shaven-

---

[81] 2 Corinthians 3:17

headed prostitution is to our modern cities, this plea is still applicable to you and me. Our modern cities may have an appearance or behavior that identifies with an idolatrous attitude. It is for our good and for the name of Jesus Christ that we identify what that is in our hometowns and separate ourselves from disgracing the name of Christ.

For some, head coverings matter in your nation. They set you apart in your identity to Christ due to the culture in which you live. Sweet Sister, set yourselves apart in the tradition of your salvation and choose to "love Jesus, evidently."

For others, it may be more difficult to identify with the image of Christ as witnessed in our cultures. What is the image of Christ? Truly, consider this question. What is the image of Christ? How can you display His image in such a way that everyone knows that you are His follower?

This question is difficult to answer. It truly is, for in answering according to our own standards of appearance, we may become tempted to pick up those stones. I hate how easy it is to cast our stones. I urge us all to truly contemplate what it is that we can portray that will allow those around us to know that we are a member of the family of God.

Here is my personal thought process: If I were to wear a head covering to my church in Eagle, Idaho, this Sunday, my head covering would not declare to my church family that I am a believer in Jesus Christ. It wouldn't. Pending my choice of head covering, it may produce questions, compliments, or distractions to those around me. Regarding my hair, I have attended multiple churches with both long and short hair. Sometimes it is brown, sometimes it is blonde. Once it was red. None of these hairstyle choices depicted my belief in Jesus to others.

I grew up hearing the age-old adage: *If the barn needs painting, paint it.* Despite my true opinion on that quote, I started wearing makeup as a teenager. Fast forward to my thirties, and a sweet lady corrected my decision telling me that I was disgraceful to the name of Christ by wearing makeup. Hmm.

I am certain that some might say that our clothing style or shoe choice or the bag that we carry or do not carry allows those around us to know that we have an intimate relationship with God. Others of us credit our word choice, our tone of voice, or the manners we properly display. Wearing a cross for some is a sweet choice. For others, wearing a cross may feel fake or forced or "religious." Image choices are endless, and opinions are everywhere. Our presentation of our physical image matters, yes. But there is not one physical image that we can all depict that would allow us all to identify with God. So again, I ask what is that image of God that we can cover ourselves with to display His image?

The answer today is the same as it was in Corinth: Submission.

Oh, how longingly you were hoping I did not say what the Lord was already whispering. But it is the truth. Our willingness to submit to the position that He created us for is the natural image to portray. Here is the beautiful piece to this truth: The image of submission is going to vary between you and me, between your city and mine, between your country and mine. Why? Because all cities, nations, and marriages have their own marks.

Behold the face of God, and let His love wash over you. Let the face of Christ shine upon you as you submit to His voice in your life. Gaze into the eyes of your husband and submit to him in a natural manner. Just as your walk with God is going to differ from my walk with God, your submission to your husband is going to differ from my submission to my husband. How beautiful is the gift of submission! When it displays its variation, the heart of the display emanates the glory of the Father equally.

Sweet Friend, this entire passage has nothing to do with our hair today, but it has everything to do with our head. That is, the head of submission. God designed it. Christ demonstrated it. It is now up to us as men and women, husbands and wives to choose to follow Christ in full submission to God. How that looks is up to each of us as we walk in faith with our God.

Scripture:

> *Judge for yourselves:*
> *is it proper for a wife to pray to God*
> *with her head uncovered?*
> *Does not nature itself teach you*
> *that if a man wears long hair*
> *it is a disgrace for him,*
> *but if a woman has long hair,*
> *it is her glory?*
> *For her hair is given to her for a covering.*
> *If anyone is inclined to be contentious,*
> *we have no such practice,*
> *nor do the churches of God.*
> *1 Corinthians 11:13–16*

Judge this matter for yourselves, Paul says. As you ponder this passage in the light of submission, remember this little truth: It is about Jesus in you. Therefore, reflect Jesus. Or should I say, love Jesus, evidently? In place of contention, let the image of Jesus Christ in *you* be the light that radiates your claim to Christ as your salvation and as your faith.

Now that submission is rooted in its rightful place, far from the rock garden, let us enter the very heart of submission: The death and resurrection of Jesus Christ.

Scripture:

> *For I received from the Lord*
> *what I also delivered to you,*
> *that the Lord Jesus*
> *on the night when he was betrayed*
> *took bread,*
> *and when he had given thanks,*
> *he broke it, and said,*
> *"This is my body, which is for you.*
> *Do this in remembrance of me."*

In the same way also
he took the cup, after supper, saying,
"This cup is the new covenant in my blood.
Do this, as often as you drink it,
in remembrance of me."

For as often as you eat this bread and drink this cup,
you proclaim the Lord's death until he comes.
1 Corinthians 11:23–26

Do this. I pray that these words are fresh in our hearts as we read such a familiar passage. Paul shares Jesus' words in this passage for us to read, remember, and do. May we submit to the Spirit of God as we read this memory, remember His purpose, and do what Jesus is asking His followers to do.

Do this. Two times Jesus tells His disciples to do something in memory of Him—as if by their actions they bring glory to His name. Share in Communion both His body and His blood. Communion is a purposed display of remembering who Jesus Christ was and what Jesus Christ did on the cross for us.

Sometimes we need to shift our perspective to grow our knowledge. We have heard this passage read in relation to communion at our churches. Church congregations hold Communion in different intervals, some a few times a year, some monthly, some weekly. But all bodies of Christ observe Communion. At least they should. Jesus demonstrated it as the New Testament covenant between Him and His followers.[82] Regardless of our frequency in Communion, this portion is one of those passages we read in a familiar memory. This is great in that we have stored His words in our hearts.[83] But not great in that we may have lost the intensity of its words, the reality of its depth.

I just left my desk to sit cross-legged on my prayer couch. This passage is too big for posture at a desk. So here I sit, reclined and curled up in His

[82] Matthew 26:26–29; Luke 22:14–23
[83] Psalm 119:11

presence to discuss His absence. Luke 22 is the largest of the three Gospel accounts of the Lord's Supper. Luke records more of Jesus' words than we see in Matthew and Mark. It is his account that draws me in relation to what we see here in 1 Corinthians 11.

> *"I have earnestly desired to eat this Passover with you before I suffer."*
> *Luke 22:15*

The intensity of Jesus' desire to partake in this last meal is powerful. Jesus has been present in the Passover since its ordination back in Exodus. In the Godhead, He was there. Throughout the wilderness, He was there. Throughout the years of tradition in the Jewish nation, in the Godhead, Jesus was there. As a child, Jesus partook of the traditional feast of the Passover.[84] Throughout His 33 years as a Jewish man, He celebrated the feast with his family and friends and nation. The Passover has been a part of Jesus for thousands of years.

Here, He sits in his humanity with his dearest friends and his betrayer. Jesus knows the feelings that are running through Peter and James and Matthew and Judas. He knows the emotions that are running through His own body: His plea to God, His prayers for us, His love for mankind, His awareness of physical pain, His reunion with Satan sitting before Him. And he expresses, *"I have earnestly desired to eat this Passover with you."* How intimate are His words! How longingly He needed this moment with them! But notice that Jesus did not consume the meal; only those present with Him did.

His desire to eat this Passover with His friends was not about the act of eating a meal but in instituting a heart of remembrance. Instituting a moment to crave.

> *"For I tell you I will not eat it until it is fulfilled in the kingdom of God."*
> *Luke 22:16*

---

[84] Luke 2:41–52

It. I love when doctrine spills out so beautifully simple. Jesus explains the beginning and the end of the traditional Passover with one little word — it. He says, "I desire to eat this Passover with you, but I will not eat *this Passover* until *this Passover* is fulfilled in the kingdom of God."

According to Jesus' words in Luke, Jesus served the elements without partaking in them. He gave up his flesh's desire until Passover was fulfilled, until His suffering was complete, until His victory song rings loudly for all the world to hear. He submitted his right to partake for God's eternal plan of salvation for you and me.

"Take this (the cup) *and divide it among yourselves.*
For I tell you that from now on I will not drink of the fruit of the vine
until the kingdom of God comes."
Luke 22:17b–18

Setting Himself aside, Jesus draws the focus on the disciples. He offers them a cup filled with wine and requests that they share in its contents. We can almost feel the confusion and obedience that passed hand to hand. We can feel the sorrow and the hope, the love and angst that traverses within each heart. And Jesus watches as each of His most beloved humans receive their portion of the wine, one after the other. He watches them divide the wine with careful respect and with eagerness to do what Jesus instructed of them.

As they obeyed his request, Jesus reminds them of His commitment to obey God's request.

"This is my body, which is given for you. Do this in remembrance of me."
Luke 22:19b

Do this. These two words have been circling my heart without finding its place of rest. The confusion must have trickled from their faces as Jesus commanded them to take broken and blessed bread and eat it. By this point in their relationship with Jesus, they have seen Him do wonders with bread. But here, He tells them to simply eat. And to remember His body as they eat.

On this day, at this meal, the mental image of Jesus' body was easy to recall. I wonder if they took mental snapshots of His eyes, His smile, or His hair. I wonder if they took note of His hands or His feet. Holding their image of this Man who sat in their midst as they chewed and consumed the bread that was broken and blessed for them.

I wonder what images remained when they gathered again after Christ's death. John's images would have altered, for he was at the foot of the cross holding and comforting the mother of Jesus.[85] The other disciples fled at His capture. Do they have images of His scarred hands and feet? Did they see the results of the forty stripes or of the crown of thorns that dripped its presence down the face of Jesus Christ, the Son of God? When they remembered His body, did they immediately picture it as it was being prepared for burial? Did they see His lifeless form lying there in the tomb before they rolled the stone to seal His death? Did they, I wonder, remember when Christ appeared in their midst three days later? I imagine Peter and James and John recognizing Him in His glorified body.[86] Perhaps, they caught a glance at one another as they remembered the Lord's body revealed in His glory.

Do this. Remember My body.

"This cup that is poured out for you is the new covenant in my blood.
But behold, the hand of him who betrays me is with me on the table.
For the Son of Man goes as it has been determined,
but woe to that man by whom he is betrayed!"
Luke 22:20b–22

Jesus interrupts their thoughts by pointing His attention back to the cup that He poured out for each of them. The same cup Jesus prayed for God to take away, *"Nevertheless, not my will but thine."* This very cup was shared among all who sat before Him. Including Judas Iscariot, the betrayer.

---

[85] John 19:26–27
[86] Matthew 17:1–13

Judas, who engaged in the partaking and the remembering of his Lord's body, sat there as the cup of wine poured out for him. Judas sat there. Judas engaged. Judas partook. Jesus makes Judas' truth known.

Scripture:

Let a person examine himself, then,
and so eat of the bread and drink of the cup.
For anyone who eats and drinks
without discerning the body
eats and drinks judgment on himself.
That is why many of you are weak and ill,
and some have died.
But if we judged ourselves truly,
we would not be judged.
But when we are judged by the Lord,
we are disciplined
so that we may not be condemned
along with the world.
So then, my brothers,
when you come together to eat,
wait for one another —
if anyone is hungry,
let him eat at home —
so that when you come together
it will not be for judgment.
1 Corinthians 11:28–34a

When you and I eat the bread and when we drink from the cup, we are remembering the body of Jesus Christ. We are remembering the blood that finalized the tradition of the Passover Feast. We are remembering the New Covenant of open communication between us and God the Father through the blood poured out for all mankind. When we eat and drink, we are doing this in remembrance of Jesus the Christ, the Son of God.

When we engage in Communion, the memory of our Lord and Savior overcomes our thoughts and emotions. And in our memory, our flesh falls at His feet. Our submission to His love pours out of us, washed anew in our memory of who He is and who we are in Him.

For Judas and for those mentioned in this Corinthian passage, something was missing. They did not *"Do This"* in memory of Jesus Christ. Again, something was missing. For us to point out each missing piece deflects the heart of our study. For all we would be doing is casting stones.

The truth is that our hearts know when something is missing, and they know what is missing. Judas knew his plan of betrayal. It had already begun.[87] Yet, still he showed up and engaged. He still ate the bread and drank the wine, but his purpose of attendance was far from the heart of remembrance.

Be honest. Be real. Be sensitive to the voice of the Spirit. Catch this truth: Communion is about Jesus. When it is not, we need to be honest with ourselves about what is causing that missing piece. We must. There really is not another way to say this. Be honest. Be real. We are adults. We know when something is missing in our relationships. Figure out what that missing piece is in your relationship with Christ Jesus. A good place to start is to truly *"Do this in remembrance of me."*

Each time we partake in Communion, we unite ourselves together in remembering His act of submission. We shed our desire to focus on the personal image *we* want to portray. Instead, we follow in His image, in His example of love, in His submission.

My prayer is that you and I will stand confident in what that looks like individually. And that we will purpose to unite together in "Doing This" in place of casting stones.

---

[87] Matthew 26:14–15

Jaclyn Palmer

Notes

1 Corinthians 12

Now concerning spiritual gifts, brothers, I do not want you to be uninformed. You know that when you were pagans you were led astray to mute idols, however you were led. Therefore I want you to understand that no one speaking in the Spirit of God ever says "Jesus is accursed!" and no one can say "Jesus is Lord" except in the Holy Spirit.

Now there are varieties of gifts, but the same Spirit; and there are varieties of service, but the same Lord; and there are varieties of activities, but it is the same God who empowers them all in everyone. To each is given the manifestation of the Spirit for the common good. For to one is given through the Spirit the utterance of wisdom, and to another the utterance of knowledge according to the same Spirit, to another faith by the same Spirit, to another gifts of healing by the one Spirit, to another the working of miracles, to another prophecy, to another the ability to distinguish between spirits, to another various kinds of tongues, to another the interpretation of tongues. All these are empowered by one and the same Spirit, who apportions to each one individually as he wills.

For just as the body is one and has many members, and all the members of the body, though many, are one body, so it is with Christ. For in one Spirit we were all baptized into one body — Jews or Greeks, slaves or free — and all were made to drink of one Spirit.

For the body does not consist of one member but of many. If the foot should say, "Because I am not a hand, I do not belong to the body," that would not make it any less a part of the body. And if the ear should say, "Because I am not an eye, I do not belong to the body," that would not make it any less a part of the body. If the whole body were an eye, where would be the sense of hearing? If the whole body were an ear, where would be the sense of smell? But as it is, God arranged the members in the body, each one of them, as he chose. If all were a single member, where would the body be? As it is, there are many parts, yet one body.

Jaclyn Palmer

The eye cannot say to the hand, "I have no need of you," nor again the head to the feet, "I have no need of you." On the contrary, the parts of the body that seem to be weaker are indispensable, and on those parts of the body that we think less honorable we bestow the greater honor, and our unpresentable parts are treated with greater modesty, which our more presentable parts do not require. But God has so composed the body, giving greater honor to the part that lacked it, that there may be no division in the body, but that the members may have the same care for one another. If one member suffers, all suffer together; if one member is honored, all rejoice together.

Now you are the body of Christ and individually members of it. And God has appointed in the church first apostles, second prophets, third teachers, then miracles, then gifts of healing, helping, administrating, and various kinds of tongues. Are all apostles? Are all prophets? Are all teachers? Do all work miracles? Do all possess gifts of healing? Do all speak with tongues? Do all interpret? But earnestly desire the higher gifts.

And I will show you a still more excellent way.

12

Jesus is the Answer

If the foot should say,
"Because I am not a hand, I do not belong to the body,"
that would not make it any less a part of the body.
1 Corinthians 12:15

I t is funny how often friends tease me each time I begin a conversation with, "I have a question." Now it has become a joke among my team. I had zero thoughts, plans or intentions in creating a new team. It was not a plan of mine. But God had a plan; therefore, today I can happily declare, "I have a team."

You see, my friend and I quickly created a source of connection for women during a mandatory time of isolation felt around the world per our church's request. My friend knew how to get things done; I knew how to teach Scripture. Together, in our polar oppositeness, we each held on tight to the mighty hand of God and jumped.

Today, there are more than thirty of us on this team with a growing list of amazing volunteers who keep connection happening within large and small groups in our city and abroad. I think about this team as I read 1 Corinthians Chapter 12. This body did not come together because there were dire positions to be filled; rather, this body came together because God had a plan. In His plan, each of us — with our unique abilities — said yes when asked to join this team. He chose each of us as we are and where we are, beautifully building up this body together. Each with her ability effortlessly complementing one another in our abilities.

This team is a lovely picture of what God designed on the sixth day of existence. These women are evidence that God is still creating beautiful things. He continues to breathe life into what He creates. And our God is still in the center of it all.

I would love to brag so deeply on each of these girls, but none of them would appreciate that. I can see them shift uncomfortably in their seats just at the thought. And I smile. I will, however, lift their voices in joint adoration to our God. We are all in complete awe at what He has done and what He is doing through our little world of Women Inseparable. It started as a "fill in the blank" Bible study via Zoom on April 2, 2020, with a small group of strangers who willingly logged on feeling all the emotions of unanswered questions. We are now an ever-growing group of women. We are women who are standing on the promise of Romans 8:35 that nothing can separate us from the love of God that is in Christ Jesus our Lord. Nothing!

My friend and I had no idea what God was doing that spring. But today we are understanding that He was doing what He has been doing for two thousand years — creating the Body of Christ and breathing life into it.

We have discussed much throughout this journey in 1 Corinthians. We have seen who we are in the love of God. We have seen and testified about the love of Jesus Christ. We have learned and embraced the need and presence of the Holy Spirit. We have looked around the church, the world, and our homes. We have seen how to use the tool of judgment properly for the growth of the Name of Jesus Christ per each individual situation. Oh, how we have discussed much within this study!

I have a question: Are you ready to join the team?

Now. Now it is time to answer the question. Yes or no. If yes, get ready to sharpen your tool of judgment that much more. What is sitting before us in these next few chapters has caused too many divisions and splits among the body of Christ. Does it not make sense that Paul chooses right here and right now to discuss the function and importance of natural unity within the physical body?

If no, thank you for being real. I pray you will read the words of Paul and pocket all that you grasp for when you are ready. Until that time, rest in your position within the body of Christ. Yes, whether you are ready to jump in or not, as a believer in Jesus Christ, you are already a part of this beautiful, intricate body. You have a place. You are a cell producing life within us as we serve in the way God has created us to serve. You have a position. And at your presence within the body of Christ, I smile. For my part is to teach. And I see you sitting, learning, growing and being. I smile at your determination to show up and sit and learn and grow and be.

Shall we gather around Paul's analogy, each of us as we are?

Scripture:

>*Now concerning spiritual gifts, brothers,*
>*I do not want you to be uninformed.*
>*You know that when you were pagans*
>*you were led astray to mute idols,*
>*however you were led.*
>*Therefore I want you to understand*
>*that no one speaking in the Spirit of God ever says,*
>*"Jesus is accursed!"*
>*and no one can say*
>*"Jesus is Lord"*
>*except in the Holy Spirit.*
>
>*Now there are varieties of gifts,*
>*but the same Spirit;*
>*and there are varieties of service,*
>*but the same Lord;*

and there are varieties of activities,
but it is the same God
who empowers them all in everyone.
1 Corinthians 12:1–6

There is a story within us that does not make complete sense. When we look back at our lives before Jesus Christ, we remember the sound of voiceless entities. The Corinthians relate to this contrast, too. Before Jesus, they could testify that something drew them to something that did not have the physical ability to draw them. Yet they drew them one way or another, as if there were a power behind the inanimate object to which they craved to listen. Can we relate?

Existing outside the body of Christ is aimlessness. It is declaring that Jesus is accursed! It is the leading astray to lifelessness. We may not have declared these words in the moment, but looking back, we see it clearly.

In contrast, Jesus! Jesus turns us around from an aimless life to a place of belonging and purpose. And He connects us into a body that testifies that Jesus is Lord and that cares for one another in the love of Jesus.

Paul uses the illustration of the physical body to open our eyes to what the body of Christ is like. The body of Christ, He says, declares that Jesus is Lord by the leading of the Holy Spirit. One Jesus. One Spirit. One body. One God.[88]

Just as your physical image is one body built together with countless pieces like bones and cells, muscles and sinews, so is this beautiful body of Christ built together with countless pieces like you and me and all those who believe in Jesus throughout this world. Nation by nation, tongue by tongue, culture by culture, ability by ability — this diverse body proclaims that Jesus is Lord. Equally and individually created by the same God, loved by the same Lord, and empowered by the same Spirit.

---

[88] Ephesians 4

Scripture:

> *To each is given the manifestation of the Spirit for the common good.*
> *For to one is given through the Spirit the utterance of wisdom,*
> *and to another the utterance of knowledge according to the same Spirit,*
> *to another faith by the same Spirit,*
> *to another gifts of healing by the one Spirit,*
> *to another the working of miracles,*
> *to another prophecy,*
> *to another the ability to distinguish between spirits,*
> *to another various kinds of tongues,*
> *to another the interpretation of tongues.*
>
> *All these are empowered by one and the same Spirit,*
> *who apportions to each one individually as he wills.*
>
> *For just as the body is one and has many members,*
> *and all the members of the body,*
> *though many, are one body,*
> *so it is with Christ.*
> *For in one Spirit we were all baptized into one body —*
> *Jews or Greeks, slaves or free —*
> *and all were made to drink of one Spirit.*
> *For the body does not consist of one member but of many.*
> *1 Corinthians 12:7–14*

Repeatedly, Paul urgently repeats this truth: You have the manifestation of the Holy Spirit for the common good of the body of Christ for the glory of God, the Creator. I have the manifestation of the Holy Spirit for the common good of the body of Christ for the glory of God, the Creator. Each person who has placed their own faith in Jesus Christ has the manifestation of the Holy Spirit for the common good of the body of Christ for the glory of God, the Creator.

Repeat.

In this repetition, we see how beautifully unique the Spirit is in His using each of us as God created us. The Spirit collaborates with God's design to deepen the message of Jesus Christ to the world around us. It is breathtaking to behold. Amazing to be a part of.

The Spirit of God gives wisdom, knowledge, and faith to those within the body of Christ as the Spirit sees fit. He gives healing, miracles, and prophecy to those within the body of Christ as the Spirit sees fit. He alone decides who distinguishes spirits, speaks in tongues, and interprets tongues within the body of Christ as He sees fit.

He gives a beautiful array of gifts to believers. Paul lists the gifts of the Spirit throughout the New Testament letters. Free tests are available online that will allow you to see where your strengths and abilities are and how He uses each within this beautiful body of Christ.

As I sit here typing out the gifts listed in this chapter right here in our study on judgment, I wonder if judgment is occurring by those of us participating in this study. Unconsciously, we gather up our doctrine stones or our comparison stones. We reach out and grab hold of our favored judgment at the mention of a passage of Scripture that does not fit in our religious dialect. Or am I the only one to admit this?

How can we beam in awe at the Holy Spirit working within us as God's design to deepen the message of Jesus Christ to the world around us and judge another for beaming at the same? It is as if we are sitting side by side enamored at the face of Jesus shining upon us as we are slapping one another like toddlers in the back of a minivan.

Judgment and division over the gifts of the Holy Spirit are not okay. May I say that again? Christians judging one another and dividing from one another because of differing opinions about the gifts of the Holy Spirit is not okay. Satan is in that division. He is causing you and me to set our eyes on one another and therefore taking our eyes off the sweet face of Jesus Christ. Oh, that these next three chapters will be a game changer for us who insist on throwing stones at the one body of Christ!

May we remember—above all individual opinions—that there is indeed one Jesus, one Spirit, one body, and one God.

Scripture:

> *If the foot should say,*
> *"Because I am not a hand,*
> *I do not belong to the body,"*
> *that would not make it any less a part of the body.*
> *And if the ear should say,*
> *"Because I am not an eye,*
> *I do not belong to the body,"*
> *that would not make it any less a part of the body.*
> *If the whole body were an eye,*
> *where would be the sense of hearing?*
> *If the whole body were an ear,*
> *where would be the sense of smell?*
> *But as it is,*
> *God arranged the members in the body,*
> *each one of them, as he chose.*
> *If all were a single member,*
> *where would the body be?*
> *As it is,*
> *there are many parts, yet one body.*
> *The eye cannot say to the hand,*
> *"I have no need of you,"*
> *nor again the head to the feet,*
> *"I have no need of you."*
> *1 Corinthians 12:15–21*

Herein lies our topic of judgment. Whether it is a conversation among "body parts" or in the quiet of our thoughts, there are times when we either feel unneeded or feel another is unnecessary. Both hurt.

So, how do we stop this judgment of the body? I suppose we ought to ponder what Jesus did as a member of this body of believers. Jesus humbled himself by taking on the form of a servant.[89] Consider this for a moment. The Creator of the universe chose to set aside His position in the Godhead to become flesh in order to relate to His favored creation. And

---

[89] Philippians 2

173

what role did He choose? The role of servant. He came to create a body for all to serve God. In His living, He created this body on earth as it is in Heaven, for, as He declared, the Kingdom of Heaven is at hand.[90] In His death, He gave His blood to be the life source that courses through this body, this family of God. Oh, the fullness of His love!

I declare that we must stop this form of theological judgment by standing side by side viewing the world around us as an opportunity to bring it into the Kingdom of God. May we not chuck stones of judgment at the Holy Spirit for manifesting a gift in a person at a set time for a specific purpose. Instead, may we pause and lift that person up in prayer that we may join the Holy Spirit in the work that He is doing.

We may say, "But I do not believe that certain gifts are manifested by the Spirit in today's society; therefore, I rightly condemn those who bring ill will to the reputation of the body of God through their self-manifested actions."

The beautiful thing about Scripture is it always gives us a simple answer. Just as the foot cannot declare itself unnecessary because it cannot do what the hand can do, neither can the eye tell the hand that it has no place in the body because the eye cannot see the hand's purpose. Oversimplified? I don't think so.

As a person with a delicate nervous system, I fully understand the frustration and exhaustion that comes when body parts refuse to communicate and function together. I know what it feels like when a body part will not respond or do its job. I know the pain that comes within my whole body when one part overcompensates. I understand the stress that affects too many members of my body when nerves swell, overextend, or tighten up so dreadfully that my body shuts down.

Paul places the analogy of a healthy physical body at a perfect place in his letter to the Corinthians. And in our individual convictions regarding gifts of the Spirit, my prayer is that we will be mindful of our physical

[90] Matthew 4:17, 10:7

bodies as we read these next three chapters together. Take your body as a personal homework challenge. Be intentional at listening to it correspond with itself. Note the communication that takes place or fails to take place due to health matters. All the while, ponder this passage regarding the members of the body of Christ.

May I briefly say this: Yes, we have a role to play in sharpening one another within this area of spiritual gifts, but can we discuss that role in the conclusion of Chapter 14? Deal?

In the meantime, as you ponder the body of Christ, your physical body, and your role in sharpening another, I suppose we ought to revisit our original question: Do you want to join the team? The Spirit is working in you as God's design to deepen the message of Jesus Christ to the world around you. Are you ready to show up and see how God has created *you* within the body of Christ?

It is breathtaking to behold. And it is utterly amazing to be a part of.

Scripture:

> *Now you are the body of Christ*
> *and individually members of it.*
> *And God has appointed in the church*
> *first apostles, second prophets, third teachers,*
> *then miracles, then gifts of healing, helping,*
> *administrating, and various kinds of tongues.*
> *Are all apostles?*
> *Are all prophets?*
> *Are all teachers?*
> *Do all work miracles?*
> *Do all possess gifts of healing?*
> *Do all speak with tongues?*
> *Do all interpret?*
> *But earnestly desire the higher gifts.*
> *And I will show you a still more excellent way.*
> *1 Corinthians 12:27–31*

With your eyes on Jesus and your thoughts on you alone (not theology, doctrine, or opinion), consider the body of Christ and the fact that you are an individual member of the body. How honoring is that? How humbling it is to be a part of something unique!

Will you allow yourself a moment to breathe in the miraculous truth of what this body represents? Take in its creation, its breath, and its intricate connection to each member. The Holy Spirit moves within it. The blood of Jesus Christ flows freely through its veins. Take time to remember who created this body. Think about the One who manifests within each member. Dwell upon the One who lived and died and lives again for every member of this precious body. Selah.

When you are ready, will you join me in beholding something even greater than the vast display of the gifts of the Spirit?

Love.

Notes

Jaclyn Palmer

1 Corinthians 13

If I speak in the tongues of men and of angels, but have not love, I am a noisy gong or a clanging cymbal. And if I have prophetic powers, and understand all mysteries and all knowledge, and if I have all faith, so as to remove mountains, but have not love, I am nothing. If I give away all I have, and if I deliver up my body to be burned, but have not love, I gain nothing.

Love is patient and kind; love does not envy or boast; it is not arrogant or rude. It does not insist on its own way; it is not irritable or resentful; it does not rejoice at wrongdoing, but rejoices with the truth. Love bears all things, believes all things, hopes all things, endures all things.

Love never ends. As for prophecies, they will pass away; as for tongues, they will cease; as for knowledge, it will pass away. For we know in part and we prophesy in part, but when the perfect comes, the partial will pass away. When I was a child, I spoke like a child, I thought like a child, I reasoned like a child. When I became a man, I gave up childish ways. For now we see in a mirror dimly, but then face to face. Now I know in part; then I shall know fully, even as I have been fully known.

So now faith, hope, and love abide, these three; but the greatest of these is love.

13

More Than Love

If I speak in the tongues of men and of angels,
but have not love,
I am a noisy gong or a clanging cymbal.
And if I have prophetic powers,
and understand all mysteries and all knowledge,
and if I have all faith,
so as to remove mountains,
but have not love,
I am nothing.
If I give away all I have,
and if I deliver up my body to be burned,
but have not love,
I gain nothing.
1 Corinthians 13:1–3

This chapter is a rite of passage in our Christian walk. Doesn't it seem so? There are those passages that we become so familiar with that we tend to see them as a resting point in our walk. I do not know if that is entirely bad. I guess if we refrain from using familiarity as a crutch but rather as a steady path, then it is good. Don't let this passage roll over your tongue and completely miss your heart, for reading His

Word without love is dull. Let us not be drab in our reading of this little chapter known for love.

With that said, may I officially begin this chapter's study by saying that this chapter is much more than love?

Without repeating all that we studied in the last chapter, allow me to simply remind us that there is value in desiring more. Remember how Paul concluded 1 Corinthians Chapter 12: *"But earnestly desire the higher gifts. And I will show you a still more excellent way."*[91] After expending an entire chapter on the various gifts given to us as children of God, he concludes with this charge to desire more in order to see a better way. What is that way?

That way is love. Press forward in your walk with the Lord. Desire more and deeper gifts from the Spirit. Pursue a grand ministry. Crave results from your work. But only if you are doing so out of the admonition and desperation of His love. Set your eyes on the heartbeat of His love, *"...the Father has sent his Son to be the Savior of the world."* [92] That is the true birthplace of love. Jesus knew the beat of love when He proclaimed, *"I am the way, and the truth, and the life. No one comes to the Father except through me."* [93] He knew the way of love. The way of love was Himself. His heartbeat given up for our life. He is the way of love that you and I are to desire more than any other gift, calling, or ministry.

It is unusual for Paul to center his words around himself. Christ is where his words point, but here we see a touch of his testimony in a very real, very intimate way. We will see his beginnings, if you will, in Chapter 15 where he declares, *"But by the grace of God I am what I am..."* [94] But here he sees himself as God has allowed him to be and who we think of him to be: a spiritual hero.

---

[91] 1 Corinthians 12:31
[92] 1 John 4:14
[93] John 14:6
[94] 1 Corinthians 15:10

Again, many of us know this passage. We know to turn to this chapter to motivate ourselves in the way of relational love. Today, I encourage you to read it slowly and bit by bit. Take each section as an inspiration to crave more than the act of love we expend upon others. Begin with the first three verses as if you are peeking into Paul's journal. As you peer, note his personal account as he centers the verb of love around his reality.

Scripture:

> *If I speak in the tongues of men and of angels,*
> *but have not love,*
> *I am a noisy gong or a clanging cymbal.*
> *And if I have prophetic powers,*
> *and understand all mysteries and all knowledge,*
> *and if I have all faith,*
> *so as to remove mountains,*
> *but have not love,*
> *I am nothing.*
> *If I give away all I have,*
> *and if I deliver up my body to be burned,*
> *but have not love,*
> *I gain nothing.*
> *1 Corinthians 13:1–3*

Paul records eight *I* statements within these three sentences. One could consider this self-promoting, but he is using himself in the same manner of submission as seen in Chapter 11. Paul was an apostle of Jesus Christ. To be an apostle of Christ, one had to witness the resurrection of Christ. Paul, in his extreme humility, exclaims that he is qualified to something too grand for him to comprehend.[95] It is in this tone, that we find 1 Corinthians Chapter 13.

Paul's testimony can compare to ours. Although, we cannot achieve status of apostleship today, we can claim Christ as our Savior; therefore, we can identify in Jesus, filled with God's Spirit, as we saw in the last chapter. Consider your own testimony as a child of God as you read

---

[95] 1 Corinthians 15:8–9

Paul's testimony. Appreciate the differences, note the similarities, and pursue the heart of love beckoning you throughout this simple chapter.

Paul's testimony:

- includes his gifts[96] of the Spirit, tongues[97] and teaching.[98]
- includes his apostolic authority: prophecy, understanding mysteries and knowledge, and mountain-moving faith.[99]
- states his present, sacrificial existence of giving it all away.[100]
- points to his expected death based on the testimony of his apostle brothers.[101]

In all these things, both highs and lows, he points to the better way: Love.

Paul begins his "I" statements by using his gifts without love as an example of a noisy gong. He is not demeaning prayerful tongues or Scriptural teaching. Rather, he is declaring the depth of inconceivable sounds when any gift is without love for the Lord. Gifts become dreadfully annoying to the hearer. Can you testify to this truth? Have you ever witnessed a spiritual leader or peer act out a gift without noticeable admiration for God? It is as if it hurts our hearts to witness it. Consider that God Almighty is our number one audience. How heartbreaking if our gift from the Spirit is a painfully empty sound in the ears of our Creator.

He then proceeds to his position in the family of God, an apostle. To be an apostle of Jesus Christ was not an ordinary position. It was a position given to certain men for a particular time in history. They had their directions, their callings, and their leadings. The twelve disciples

---

[96] Romans 12; 1 Corinthians 12
[97] 1 Corinthians 14:18
[98] 1 Corinthians 14:6, 19
[99] Acts 9:15, 1-19, 26:15–18
[100] 2 Corinthians 11:22-32
[101] 2 Timothy 4:6-8, 17-18

stood as apostles of Jesus alongside Paul.[102] Imagine if Peter, James, Matthew, or Paul attempted to perform the power poured into them by the Holy Spirit without love for their Lord Jesus. The very thought is oxymoronic. Paul declares worthlessness above all measure if he dared to display apostolic authority without love.

Lastly, he says, that when he dies a martyr's death, let his death be full of glory to the King of kings. But if he dies for Christ without love for Christ, oh, that he would gain nothing! When you hear that spelled out in this chapter, does your heart not burn for Galatians 2:20? To die for Christ was an ever-present thought on Paul's heart. Not because he craved for us to remember how he died for Christ, but that he walked in the steps of Christ and is now in the presence of his Savior. Love is the better way even in death.

May we look at our testimony in the same manner as Paul viewed his. May we behold our gifts from the Spirit with the intention of pursuing the way of love. May we see our position within the family of God as an opportunity to display the way of love. And may we give all that the Lord is asking of us for the purpose of love.

Yes, desire more from the Lord. But base your desire on the love of the Father demonstrated by the Son and grown through the Spirit. Love: It is the better way.

Scripture:

> *Love is patient and kind;*
> *love does not envy or boast;*
> *it is not arrogant or rude.*
> *It does not insist on its own way;*
> *it is not irritable or resentful;*
> *it does not rejoice at wrongdoing,*
> *but rejoices with the truth.*
> *Love bears all things,*

---

[102] 1 Corinthians 15:5–9

believes all things,
hopes all things,
endures all things.
Love never ends.
1 Corinthians 13:4–8a

God's love has a beginning without an end. Allow this truth to wash over you. Take a moment to remember when His love began in you. Remember the moment you declared your need for a Savior and your desire for a Father. Remember the feeling of love covering you. And thank the Lord for His everlasting love. Thank Him for not limiting His love pending your life lessons or pending your death. Oh, how He loves you. I would even encourage you to pen your memory of His love. Record the day you fell in love with His love. If you do take a moment to write down your testimony, you may find yourself falling in love with Christ even more.

Paul met love on the road to Damascus.[103] His story is dynamic. But in all his recounting of his story, he rarely discusses his *before*. He would much rather tell of the love of Jesus Christ, the risen Son of God. For it is the love of Jesus that turned his life right side up. It is Jesus' love that changed the course of his life, his purpose, his love, and his death.

Christ's love plants itself within us. It blooms and blossoms deep within our core stirring our every dream, every goal, every victory, every sorrow to point to the love of Jesus Christ. This love does not end at death, for death has no sting. It has no victory.[104] Love carries us into the presence of God Almighty. Can you imagine the depth of love that will encircle us that day?

Love never ends. How this thought causes my heart to sing, my lips to smile, and my love to grow. We are forever loved and in love with our God. This love is a gift given to us, freely. Take a moment to ponder the evidence of His love for you. Oh, how He loves you! From the moment

---

[103] Acts 9:1–9
[104] 1 Corinthians 15:55

He created you, to the moment you understood your need for His love, and to the day that love welcomes you to your home in eternity, His love never fails!

Often, we dwell on the attributes of our love in comparison to verses 4–8. I pray we will reread these simple verses in the light of the better way, considering the love of Jesus Christ. John, both an apostle and disciple of Jesus Christ, wrote a beautiful depiction of the way love flows from God to Christ to you and me. It is poetic and abundantly applicable to our study today. Listen to the heart of John's words:

> .... *God is love.*
> *In this the love of God was made manifest among us,*
> *that God sent His only Son into the world,*
> *so that we might live through him.*
> *In this is love,*
> *not that we have loved God but that he loved us*
> *and sent His Son to be the propitiation for our sins.*
> *Beloved, if God so loved us,*
> *we also ought to love one another.*
> *1 John 4:8b–11*

Love threads 1 Corinthians Chapters 12–14 together with intentionality. These three chapters link seamlessly with love. How I desire that our eyes will be open to the thread of Jesus' blood that links us together when controversy tries to pull us apart.

Again, we see intentionality in Paul's connection to the way of love dipped within the context of these topics. Consider the length of space Paul uses in this letter to the Corinthians regarding these issues. Remembering that he wrote this as a letter without chapters and verses, we easily see that a fifth of this letter focuses on these matters. Clearly — it was a hot topic then as it is today. Let us sit with our church family of long ago and listen to the heart of Paul's message. Let us gather the information we learned in the last chapter and fill ourselves with the love of Christ before jumping into the next chapter.

An open discussion on prophecy and tongues will meet us in 1 Corinthians Chapter 14, but let us first understand these gifts in light of God's love. If you found your heart reaching for a stone at the mention of prophecy and tongues, will you pause and, once again, meditate on 1 John 4? Perhaps you need to join me on your knees with 1 John 4 open before the Throne. There is room beside me there.

Scripture:

> *Love never ends.*
> *As for prophecies,*
> *they will pass away;*
> *as for tongues,*
> *they will cease;*
> *as for knowledge,*
> *it will pass away.*
> *For we know in part*
> *and we prophesy in part,*
> *but when the perfect comes,*
> *the partial will pass away.*
> *1 Corinthians 13:8–10*

Love never ends. However, prophecy does have an expiration date — as do the speaking of tongues and the gift of knowledge. Setting the debate aside as to when that expiration date was or is to come, this passage declares its end. The Spirit gave these three things for a purpose in a specific time and for a specific reason. Once accomplished, they will cease to exist. According to this passage, prophecies and knowledge will pass away and tongues will cease. It will happen. In this, there is no question.

Also, according to this passage, we know that we do not know all the things. We may understand in part, but we will not see the full picture until we fully know God Almighty in Heaven. At that time, we will know God with the entirety in which He knows us. In this, we will finally behold the fullness of prophecies, tongues, and knowledge.

For you see, these three things become void in the presence of God. There will be a day when these will not be needed. For when this day comes, we will no longer see only half the picture. Instead, the mighty presence of the Father will fully embrace us. And in His presence, we will see the full mystery of the Spirit of God.

Some say that prophecy and tongues have ceased since the publication of the written Word. While others declare that prophecy and tongues are essential to the Christian life today. Furthermore, we are all aware that the topic of prophecy and tongues is a hot topic full of strongly stated convictions. Therefore, I will not state my opinion on these topics, and I ask that you set your opinion on a windowsill for just a quick minute. Together, may we remember that God has their expiration date marked in Heaven.

My goal is that we will sit side-by-side in the reading of Scripture without engaging in a stone war as if we were children. Not my words, mind you, Paul's.

Scripture:

> *When I was a child,*
> *I spoke like a child,*
> *I thought like a child,*
> *I reasoned like a child.*
> *When I became a man,*
> *I gave up childish ways.*
> *For now we see in a mirror dimly,*
> *But then face to face.*
> *Now I know in part;*
> *then I shall know fully,*
> *even as I have been fully known.*
> *1 Corinthians 13:11–12*

Repeatedly, I heard that I perceive things as a child and one day I will understand as an adult. This was the passage quoted to me when I had questions regarding man-made laws versus Scripture. I sit here today blown away at the context of this passage. It has nothing to do with understanding the law of man. Rather, it has everything to do with understanding our position as a human in the realm of the Heavenly.

Just as we learn how to be a member of the body of Christ by studying the unification of the human body, we also learn the similarities of Christian growth in comparison with human growth. Catch Paul's words in the context of this passage. He is not belittling the limited knowledge of a child. Rather, he is exemplifying a child's limited knowledge as natural. Then he further explains the limited knowledge of man. Not in a belittling manner, but in full explanation that as an adult we naturally know more than we did as a child. Furthermore, just as we graduated in child-like knowledge to adult-level expertise, so will we graduate from human adult to our resurrected glory. Knowledge will max out.

How I cannot wait for that day! As a child, I wanted more than anything for others to perceive me as smart. I checked out any big book I could get each time I visited the library. I grabbed books that would define me as a smart girl despite my lack of formal education. When I was 12 years old, my Sunday School teacher encouraged me to pray for wisdom every day. He told me that God wants me to pray for wisdom, so He could give me an abundance of wisdom.[105] I was thrilled. And I prayed. Daily. I have not stopped praying for wisdom since that day.

I know things. I have learned things through natural maturing, through reading, and through God's promise of wisdom. But one day, I will know everything. This truth blows my mind. My greatest desire will happen on that day when I stand before the very God who created me to have this desire. Full circle in love with the Heavenly Father simply because He loved me first and called me His.

Paul understood his limitation. Using himself, despite his spiritual status, Paul says, "*When I was a child, I spoke like a child, I thought like a child, I reasoned like a child. When I became a man, I gave up childish ways.*" (v.11) This is simple truth at its finest. The question is why he chose to place this

---

[105] James 1:5

remark here. The simple verbal expression points us to the answer. *"For now we see in a mirror dimly, but then face to face. Now I know in part; then I shall know fully, even as I have been fully known."* (v.12) Ah, simple truth dipped in deep theology!

If you and I believe in the resurrecting power of Jesus Christ, then you and I can stand with Paul in his declaration of understanding. We, too, can understand that our adult knowledge is greater than our child-like knowledge. And we can stand with Paul, understanding the limitations of our adult knowledge, knowing that one day we will know God as God knows us.

One day — what a glorious day that will be!

Scripture:

> *So now faith, hope, and love abide,*
> *these three;*
> *but the greatest of these is love.*
> *1 Corinthians 13:13*

Prophecies, tongues, and knowledge will cease to exist. Faith, hope, and love never will. My prayer is that we will put the proper emphasis into each of these but that we will always remember that only one of these things is defined as the greatest of all. This is the better way. This is love.

Notes

_____
_____
_____
_____
_____
_____
_____
_____
_____
_____
_____
_____
_____
_____
_____
_____
_____
_____
_____
_____
_____
_____
_____
_____
_____
_____
_____

1 Corinthians 14

*Pursue love, and earnestly desire the spiritual gifts, especially that you
may prophesy. For one who speaks in a tongue speaks not to men but to
God; for no one understands him, but he utters mysteries in the Spirit.
On the other hand, the one who prophesies speaks to people for their
upbuilding and encouragement and consolation. The one who speaks in
a tongue builds up himself, but the one who prophesies builds up the church.
Now I want you all to speak in tongues, but even more to prophesy.
The one who prophesies is greater than the one who speaks in tongues,
unless someone interprets, so that the church may be built up.*

*Now, brothers, if I come to you speaking in tongues, how will I benefit
you unless I bring you some revelation or knowledge or prophecy or teaching?
If even lifeless instruments, such as the flute or the harp, do not give distinct
notes, how will anyone know what is played? And if the bugle gives an
indistinct sound, who will get ready for battle? So with yourselves, if with
your tongue you utter speech that is not intelligible, how will anyone know
what is said? For you will be speaking into the air. There are doubtless many
different languages in the world, and none is without meaning, but if I do not
know the meaning of the language, I will be a foreigner to the speaker and the
speaker a foreigner to me. So with yourselves, since you are eager for
manifestations of the Spirit, strive to excel in building up the church.*

*Therefore, one who speaks in a tongue should pray that he may interpret.
For if I pray in a tongue, my spirit prays but my mind is unfruitful. What am I
to do? I will pray with my spirit, but I will pray with my mind also; I will sing
praise with my spirit, but I will sing with my mind also. Otherwise, if you give
thanks with your spirit, how can anyone in the position of an outsider say
"Amen" to your thanksgiving when he does not know what you are saying?
For you may be giving thanks well enough, but the other person is not being
built up. I thank God that I speak in tongues more than all of you.*

Nevertheless, in church I would rather speak five words with my mind in order to instruct others, than ten thousand words in a tongue.

Brothers, do not be children in your thinking. Be infants in evil, but in your thinking be mature. In the Law it is written, "By people of strange tongues and by the lips of foreigners will I speak to this people, and even then they will not listen to me, says the Lord." Thus tongues are a sign not for believers but for unbelievers, while prophecy is a sign not for unbelievers but for believers. If, therefore, the whole church comes together and all speak in tongues, and outsiders or unbelievers enter, will they not say that you are out of your minds? But if all prophesy, and an unbeliever or outsider enters, he is convicted by all, he is called to account by all, the secrets of his heart are disclosed, and so, falling on his face, he will worship God and declare that God is really among you.

What then, brothers? When you come together, each one has a hymn, a lesson, a revelation, a tongue, or an interpretation. Let all things be done for building up. If any speak in a tongue, let there be only two or at most three, and each in turn, and let someone interpret. But if there is no one to interpret, let each of them keep silent in church and speak to himself and to God. Let two or three prophets speak, and let the others weigh what is said. If a revelation is made to another sitting there, let the first be silent. For you can all prophesy one by one, so that all may learn and all be encouraged, and the spirits of prophets are subject to prophets. For God is not a God of confusion but of peace.

As in all the churches of the saints, the women should keep silent in the churches. For they are not permitted to speak, but should be in submission, as the Law also says. If there is anything they desire to learn, let them ask their husbands at home. For it is shameful for a woman to speak in church.

Or was it from you that the word of God came? Or are you the only ones it has reached? If anyone thinks that he is a prophet, or spiritual, he should acknowledge that the things I am writing to you are a command of the Lord. If anyone does not recognize this, he is not recognized. So, my brothers, earnestly desire to prophesy, and do not forbid speaking in tongues. But all things should be done decently and in order.

14

One Vital Truth

Pursue love,
and earnestly desire the spiritual gifts...
since you are eager for manifestations of the Spirit,
strive to excel in building up the church.
1 Corinthians 14:1a, 12

Y ou and I made a deal in Chapter 12. My prayer is that we will reach our answer by the end of this chapter at hand. I pray also that we will not engage in a stone war as we read Scripture together today. May we keep love at the forefront of our minds as we sit in Paul's words.

Scripture:

Pursue love,
and earnestly desire the spiritual gifts,
especially that you may prophesy.
For one who speaks in a tongue
speaks not to men but to God;
for no one understands him,
but he utters mysteries in the Spirit.

On the other hand,
the one who prophesies
speaks to people for their upbuilding
and encouragement and consolation.
The one who speaks in a tongue builds up himself,
but the one who prophesies builds up the church.

Now I want you all to speak in tongues,
but even more to prophesy.
The one who prophesies is greater
than the one who speaks in tongues,
unless someone interprets,
so that the church may be built up.
1 Corinthians 14:1–5

Do you remember 1 Corinthians Chapter 3 where Paul declares truths about the grace of God regarding our work? He exhorts us with a strong charge that is highly advisable as we set our gaze upon this chapter. *"Let each one,"* he says, *"take care how he builds upon it. For no one can lay a foundation other than that which is laid, which is Jesus Christ…and the fire will test what sort of work each one has done."*[106] On that Day, He will give a reward to you if your work proves faithful in His eyes. Alike, on that Day, He will burn your work if He sees it as useless in building up the church, the body of Christ.

One thing must be clear as we keep the tool of judgment on the table: There is only One who judges our work in the end. One. That One is not me, and it is not you. We can sharpen one another as the Spirit wills us (not when our opinion gets tripped), but we ought not ever judge one another's work in building the church. All too often, we are judging the Holy Spirit. Let us not ever be known as one who judges the very Spirit of God.

May I be so bold as to declare this truth over such divisive gifts such as tongues and prophecy? We are not God, we are not the Spirit, we are not Jesus, nor are we the Creator of the body. You and I are members of

[106] 1 Corinthians 3:10b–13

the body of Christ, created by God, loved by Jesus, and filled with the Spirit. That is who we are. And that is who all members of the body of Christ are. We must remember this vital truth, especially when it comes to our differing opinions regarding Spiritual gifts.

Jesus teaches the disciples to focus on their work for the Kingdom regardless of those around them. In Mark 9, the disciples saw a stranger casting out demons in the name of Jesus and tried to stop him. This encounter unnerved the disciples. But Jesus spoke a truth that we must process and root within us today. *"Do not stop him, for no one who does a mighty work in my name will be able soon afterward to speak evil of me."*[107] Remember: The Holy Spirit will soon use that mighty work for the furtherance of the gospel.

One thing I always need to remind myself is that our God does not need me to protect Him. Like the disciples, I so easily want to navigate a situation back to the safety of my knowledge of God. But my God is so big. Catch that. God is so much greater than our knowledge of God. He is I AM. If someone speaks the name of Jesus, God can manage that situation and can use that situation. Trust Him to be God, fully. Truthfully speaking, God is going to be God, completely, whether you trust Him to be or not. And our amazing God is going to use the Spirit's gift despite your trust in Him to use someone who differs from you.

That is how big our God is. He is I AM. Selah.

Scripture:

Pursue love,
and earnestly desire the spiritual gifts,
especially that you may prophesy.
For one who speaks in a tongue
speaks not to men but to God;
for no one understands him,
but he utters mysteries in the Spirit.

---

[107] Mark 9:39

On the other hand,
the one who prophesies
speaks to people for their upbuilding
and encouragement and consolation.
The one who speaks in a tongue builds up himself,
but the one who prophesies builds up the church.

Now I want you all to speak in tongues,
but even more to prophesy.
The one who prophesies is greater
than the one who speaks in tongues,
unless someone interprets,
so that the church may be built up.
1 Corinthians 14:1–5

Now let us look at the words of this passage without feathers flying, shall we? Also, may I insert a personal thank you to each of you for working this through with me? May we not avoid uneasy passages of God's Word, and may we never use Scripture as stones. Oh, may we never use Scripture as stones! Heartbreaking damage comes from that behavior, every time. So, thank you for studying these words with me as we, together, "pursue love."

This entire chapter is all about the two gifts of tongues and prophecy. I thought about splitting the chapter (by verses) into a tongues study and a prophecy study, but as you read the chapter, they truly intertwine. This may be why God had Paul write this letter as he did. Imagine that.

Both are gifts from the Spirit of God for the common good of the body of Christ. We see that truth in 1 Corinthians Chapter 12. Here, Paul details the very purpose of these gifts.

- Tongues is a gift between an individual and God on a personal, relational level—given by the Spirit for the building up of that person. And the Spirit hears the connection expressed during that time together. Lastly, according to the text above, to speak in tongues in a public setting will only build up others upon interpretation.

- Prophecy is a gift given to an individual for the connection between the body of Christ and God on a public, relational level — given by the Spirit for the building up of the church. The words expressed are for the growth, encouragement, and consolation/comfort of the hearer(s).

With Paul's foundation laid down, let us move on.

Scripture:

Now, brothers,
if I come to you speaking in tongues,
how will I benefit you
unless I bring you some revelation
or knowledge or prophecy or teaching?
If even lifeless instruments,
such as the flute or the harp,
do not give distinct notes,
how will anyone know what is played?
And if the bugle gives an indistinct sound,
who will get ready for battle?

So with yourselves,
if with your tongue you utter speech
that is not intelligible,
how will anyone know what is said?
For you will be speaking into the air.
1 Corinthians 14:6–9

Consider the book of Psalms as you read this text. Although the Psalmist does not give the chords behind each song, these words were all melodies penned for the ears of Almighty God. Men, such as Asaph, served God through instrumental worship.[108] The vitality of their service impacted the heart of God and the hearts of the Israelites. Each

---

[108] 1 Chronicles 6:31-32, 39; 15:17, 19; 16:4-7; 2 Chronicles 29:30

instrument has its singular value. Each one used in accordance with its own design.

Secondly, consider Gideon and his instrument of battle.[109] As you read the account of Gideon and his army of three hundred men, do you hear the united worship in their belief that God has gone before and has already won the battle that lay before them? Together, they raised their battle cry through their "battle horn."

Every instrument has its place, but it must play in tune. Even those of us who are not musically inclined shudder when an instrument is off key. It, all too easily, distracts us, the responders, from thinking about God during worship as we find ourselves focused on whoever is out of tune. This is what Paul is alluding to with this visual.

When we use our gifts outside God's design, we only bring attention to ourselves, even if unintentionally. Remember, the purpose of all gifts, the purpose of you and me, is for the common good of the body of Christ to bring glory to God, the Creator. May we see ourselves and our gifts as instruments of righteousness fit in the Master's hand.[110]

In comparison to an ill-timed instrument, Paul states that the ill-timed tongue produces the same effect on the hearts of those around us. This may be hard for our ears to hear, but are we willing to see what Paul is saying on behalf of the universal church? Paul, as one who speaks in tongues, is proclaiming the proper time and place for such a gift of the Spirit.

Friend, if your heart is dying to speak publicly in tongues, I encourage you to spend time on your knees with 1 Corinthians 3 and 14. Seek His will for your gift—not your will. Go forward in service. Just as Jesus humbled himself and became a servant, will you follow Jesus and serve? My prayer is that you will see your place in the body and that your place

[109] Judges 7:1–22
[110] Romans 6:13

will sweetly benefit those around you and increase. May the passage below resonate within your spirit.

Scripture:

There are doubtless many different languages in the world,
and none is without meaning,
but if I do not know the meaning of the language,
I will be a foreigner to the speaker
and the speaker a foreigner to me.
So with yourselves,
Since you are eager for manifestations of the Spirit,
Strive to excel in building up the church.
1 Corinthians 14:10–19

Some of us scoff at this gift of tongues. We wash over this passage with Scriptures that defend our theology of the matter. To those of us with this conviction, permit me the opportunity to remember who the Author of this passage is. It is as all Scripture, God-breathed.[111] May we be willing to step aside for a moment in honor and respect to our God who orchestrates all things for His glory and for His purpose. Who are we to squelch the overwhelming work of the Creator? We are mere instruments fit for His breath within us. I pray we will not diminish His breath with our words of judgment.

Scripture:

Brothers, do not be children in your thinking.
Be infants in evil,
but in your thinking be mature.
In the Law it is written,
"By people of strange tongues
and by the lips of foreigners
will I speak to this people,
and even then they will not listen to me,
says the Lord."

---

[111] 2 Timothy 3:16

Thus tongues are a sign not for believers
but for unbelievers,
while prophecy is a sign not for unbelievers
but for believers.
If, therefore, the whole church comes together
and all speak in tongues,
and outsiders or unbelievers enter,
will they not say that you are out of your minds?
But if all prophesy,
and an unbeliever or outsider enters,
he is convicted by all,
he is called to account by all,
the secrets of his heart are disclosed,
and so, falling on his face,
he will worship God
and declare that God is really among you.
1 Corinthians 14:20–25

How beautiful is the conclusion to this matter! Oh, that we use the gifts of the Spirit for the salvation of one more lost soul! Listen to the simplistic power found in these verses.... The Spirit uses the gift of tongues as a sign for an unsaved person, privately, whereas He uses the gift of prophecy as a sign for a believer, publicly. Do you see how the Spirit works within the body? He draws us to Him through His own conversation within our souls. This encounter is different for each of us. And that is not a terrible thing. It is a sign of a personal relationship with God. Then, as we respond to that intimate drawing of the Spirit and enter a public gathering of Christian believers, those using *their* gifts help draw us closer still to Jesus Christ. How powerful is this truth!

Oh, that another may declare that *"God is really among [us]"* (v.25) as we remain faithful in pouring out the gift the Spirit is pouring within each of us as we are!

What more is there to say? With our judgment set aside and our eyes set on Jesus, I find myself without another word to say. The Author of

Life settles all disputes within the body and within us. How good is the sweet name of Jesus!

Paul, however, has a grand way of closing out these last three chapters. Through the *"command of the Lord,"* (v.37) he settles any remaining disputes that may linger within our thoughts. Here is what he says about the unifying of the body of Christ as we learn and grow into the gift entrusted us by the Spirit of God.

Scripture:

What then, brothers?
When you come together,
each one has a hymn, a lesson, a revelation,
a tongue, or an interpretation.
Let all things be done for building up.
If any speak in a tongue,
let there be only two or at most three,
and each in turn,
and let someone interpret.
But if there is no one to interpret,
let each of them keep silent in church
and speak to himself and to God.

Let two or three prophets speak,
and let the others weigh what is said.
If a revelation is made to another sitting there,
let the first be silent.
For you can all prophesy one by one,
so that all may learn and all be encouraged,
and the spirits of prophets are subject to prophets.
For God is not a God of confusion but of peace.

As in all the churches of the saints,
the women should keep silent in the churches.
For they are not permitted to speak,
but should be in submission,
as the Law also says.

Jaclyn Palmer

If there is anything they desire to learn,
let them ask their husbands at home.
For it is shameful for a woman to speak in church.
1 Corinthians 14:26–35

At this passage, I smile. The surge of emotion that courses through the female brain is interesting. I do not know if it is the rule placed over us that bothers us or the word submission stamped upon our foreheads. Either way, this passage tends to tick off women, does it not? And, yet, as I sit here reading this passage in its context, I smile. Here's why:

God orchestrated a plan. From the creation of the body of man to the creation of the body of Christ, God had a plan and a purpose. The fullness of His masterpiece leads the world to Jesus. Catch this truth: the Father sent Jesus to Earth, Jesus ascended, then God sent the Spirit. In each "sending," submission to God's plan was involved. Both Jesus and the Spirit said yes so that salvation would abound.

God created mankind to need one another, so that together life would multiply upon the Earth. God created man to lead; He created woman to birth life. A man leads. A woman grows life. Will we pause to ponder the significance of each design?

We must willingly submit to God's plan for our design. Imagine if the lost around us find Christ through our simple willingness to follow Jesus and the Holy Spirit in their submission to the Father.

When a woman stands up to take the position of a man it is the same as when a hand takes the position of a foot. Hands can do the job of feet. We have all witnessed someone magically walking on their hands — for lengthy periods of time. But as the hands are stepping out what happens to the feet? They become weak.

And now I am praying that you are smiling, too. Truly, I do pray that the divisiveness that stirs up from these culturally unaccepted verses will dissipate in the truth of Jesus Christ. I pray that we as women will rise to our creation and hold fast to our place in the orchestra that is the body of

Christ. Consider how much more the Holy Spirit can work in us if we first humble ourselves, submit to God, and fully embrace our very design — woman.

Scripture:

> *Or was it from you that the word of God came?*
> *Or are you the only ones it has reached?*
> *If anyone thinks that he is a prophet, or spiritual,*
> *he should acknowledge*
> *that the things I am writing to you*
> *are a command of the Lord.*
> *If anyone does not recognize this,*
> *he is not recognized.*
> *So, my brothers, earnestly desire to prophesy,*
> *and do not forbid speaking in tongues.*
> *But all things should be done decently and in order.*
> *1 Corinthians 14:36–40*

As for our deal from Chapter 12, have you found your answer regarding your place in the body of Christ? And are you ready to use it for the upbuilding of the house of God? Paul is quite brazen in his final words of authority. This message, he says, is from God. No questions asked. The gifts of the Spirit are bigger than an individual's grasp of the gifts. Period. And if any of us find within ourselves the knowledge of our gift from the Spirit, we must acknowledge every gift is about Jesus, only. If we do not recognize this, then our gifts, Paul declares, are void within the body. What a clear insight on false gifts and false teaching.

When in doubt about your gift or the gift within another, check the evidence of the name of Jesus and His resurrection for the salvation of mankind. If salvation is evident, let us not judge the Holy Spirit. If attention is all about the instrument and not the breath of God, then use your spiritual judgment to protect the body from falling astray from Jesus Christ, our Risen Savior.

We do have a vital role to play in sharpening one another within this area of spiritual gifts. My role is to read Scripture aloud. I pray that is what I did throughout this book and each time I teach, for that matter. What about you? Do you see your role in sharpening another in the way of Spiritual gifts? If you were able to clearly see your role, then stand up and do what the Spirit has led you to do for the common good of the body of Christ. If you do not know what your role is in sharpening another person, great. Now allow the Spirit to sharpen you as He sees fit. Keep your eyes on Jesus and watch the Spirit do what He alone desires to do in and through you.

Isn't the body of Christ truly a beautiful creation to behold?

Oh, how wonderful it is to be a part of such a grand design!

Notes

Jaclyn Palmer

1 Corinthians 15

Now I would remind you, brothers, of the gospel I preached to you, which you received, in which you stand, and by which you are being saved, if you hold fast to the word I preached to you — unless you believed in vain.

For I delivered to you as of first importance what I also received: that Christ died for our sins in accordance with the Scriptures, that he was buried, that he was raised on the third day in accordance with the Scriptures, and that he appeared to Cephas, then to the twelve. Then he appeared to more than five hundred brothers at one time, most of whom are still alive, though some have fallen asleep. Then he appeared to James, then to all the apostles. Last of all, as to one untimely born, he appeared also to me. For I am the least of the apostles, unworthy to be called an apostle, because I persecuted the church of God. But by the grace of God I am what I am, and his grace toward me was not in vain. On the contrary, I worked harder than any of them, though it was not I, but the grace of God that is with me. Whether then it was I or they, so we preach and so you believed.

Now if Christ is proclaimed as raised from the dead, how can some of you say that there is no resurrection of the dead? But if there is no resurrection of the dead, then not even Christ has been raised. And if Christ has not been raised, then our preaching is in vain and your faith is in vain. We are even found to be misrepresenting God, because we testified about God that he raised Christ, whom he did not raise if it is true that the dead are not raised. For if the dead are not raised, not even Christ has been raised. And if Christ has not been raised, your faith is futile and you are still in your sins. Then those also who have fallen asleep in Christ have perished. If in Christ we have hope in this life only, we are of all people most to be pitied.

But in fact Christ has been raised from the dead, the firstfruits of those who have fallen asleep. For as by a man came death, by a man has come also the resurrection of the dead. For as in Adam all die, so also in Christ shall all be made alive. But each in his own order: Christ the firstfruits, then at his coming those who belong to Christ. Then comes the end, when he delivers the kingdom to God the Father after destroying every rule and every authority and power. For he must reign until he has put all his enemies under his feet. The last enemy to be destroyed is death. For "God has put all things in subjection under his feet." But when it says, "all things are put in subjection," it is plain that he is excepted who put all things in subjection under him. When all things are subjected to him, then the Son himself will also be subjected to him who put all things in subjection under him, that God may be all in all.

Otherwise, what do people mean by being baptized on behalf of the dead? If the dead are not raised at all, why are people baptized on their behalf? Why are we in danger every hour? I protest, brothers, by my pride in you, which I have in Christ Jesus our Lord, I die every day! What do I gain if, humanly speaking, I fought with beasts at Ephesus? If the dead are not raised, "Let us eat and drink, for tomorrow we die." Do not be deceived: "Bad company ruins good morals." Wake up from your drunken stupor, as is right, and do not go on sinning. For some have no knowledge of God. I say this to your shame.

But someone will ask, "How are the dead raised? With what kind of body do they come?" You foolish person! What you sow does not come to life unless it dies. And what you sow is not the body that is to be, but a bare kernel, perhaps of wheat or of some other grain. But God gives it a body as he has chosen, and to each kind of seed its own body. For not all flesh is the same, but there is one kind for humans, another for animals, another for birds, and another for fish. There are heavenly bodies and earthly bodies, but the glory of the heavenly is of one kind, and the glory of the earthly is of another. There is one glory of the sun, and another glory of the moon, and another glory of the stars; for star differs from star in glory.

So is it with the resurrection of the dead. What is sown is perishable; what is raised is imperishable. It is sown in dishonor; it is raised in glory. It is sown in weakness; it is raised in power. It is sown a natural body; it is raised a spiritual body. If there is a natural body, there is also a spiritual body. Thus it is written, "The first man Adam became a living being"; the last Adam became a life-giving spirit. But it is not the spiritual that is first but the natural, and then the spiritual. The first man was from the earth, a man of dust; the second man is from heaven. As was the man of dust, so also are those who are of the dust, and as is the man of heaven, so also are those who are of heaven. Just as we have borne the image of the man of dust, we shall also bear the image of the man of heaven.

I tell you this, brothers: flesh and blood cannot inherit the kingdom of God, nor does the perishable inherit the imperishable. Behold! I tell you a mystery. We shall not all sleep, but we shall all be changed, in a moment, in the twinkling of an eye, at the last trumpet. For the trumpet will sound, and the dead will be raised imperishable, and we shall be changed. For this perishable body must put on the imperishable, and this mortal body must put on immortality. When the perishable puts on the imperishable, and the mortal puts on immortality, then shall come to pass the saying that is written:

"Death is swallowed up in victory."
"O death, where is your victory?
O death, where is your sting?"

The sting of death is sin, and the power of sin is the law. But thanks be to God, who gives us the victory through our Lord Jesus Christ.

Therefore, my beloved brothers, be steadfast, immovable, always abounding in the work of the Lord, knowing that in the Lord your labor is not in vain.

15

An Immeasurable Truth

Now I would remind you, brothers,
of the gospel I preached to you,
which you received,
in which you stand,
and by which you are being saved,
if you hold fast to the word I preached to you —
unless you believed in vain.
Therefore, my beloved brothers,
be steadfast, immovable,
always abounding in the work of the Lord,
knowing that in the Lord your labor is not in vain.
1 Corinthians 15:1, 2, 58

I f by this point of Paul's letter, you are wondering if it is worth caring about the souls of those around us, then this chapter is for you. We just walked through fourteen chapters of lessons regarding who Jesus is, who you are, how to love the family of God, how to live for salvation of the unsaved, and how to know and do all of the above without casting and receiving stones of judgment.

Now we stand before this 58-verse chapter and wonder, "Why didn't Paul just lead with this?"

May I introduce you to a woman named Judy? She cheats. I have known this truth about her for years. I shake my head at her cheating tendencies repeatedly. We have the same hobby, but she just cheats. Every time. Just the other night, I was talking to my husband about Judy and her cheating habits. We shook our heads and laughed.

Her habit is not harmful to anyone. She is not cheating on her husband of 50 years. She is not cheating on life. She is not cheating on her taxes. Again, her habit is not harmful. But it is real. And it is hysterical. I do not get it. I have never understood why she cheats the way she does. That is until I sat with Paul's fifteenth chapter, and I caught a glimpse of the benefit of Judy's habitual cheating.

Judy is my mother-in-law. I know her well, and I love her severely. She and I are both avid readers. We just read differently. You see, when I read a book, I begin in Chapter 1 then proceed numerically throughout the novel. Judy, however, begins with the last chapter then proceeds to Chapter 1 and sees her way safely through the novel once she knows the end.

I am telling you, she cheats, and she likes it that way. When we chatted about her habit, she explained to me, "It makes me understand details as I read."

Enter 1 Corinthians Chapter 15! Judy's explanations of her reading habit resonate with the summary of this chapter in my heart. If I were Judy's personal author, I would choose to put this chapter last, so she can get right to the good stuff.

Jesus' resurrection makes us understand details as we read, walk, serve, love and live. An extensive chapter on resurrection at the conclusion of his detailed letter serves as a true and lasting reminder that the resurrection of our Lord Jesus Christ is the end-all of our faith. If it were not, then all that we have learned, loved, and performed is in vain.

Christ's love is bigger than religious vanity.

Scripture:

> *For I delivered to you as of first importance what I also received:*
> *that Christ died for our sins in accordance with the Scriptures,*
> *that he was buried, that he was raised on the third day*
> *in accordance with the Scriptures,*
> *and that he appeared to...*
> *1 Corinthians 15:3–5a*

The end matters more than the beginning, for the end ties the whole story together. The end explains the heart of the story. The end solidifies all the mysteries that stand between the dash of the stories of our life. The end matters.

Paul points out that he knows the end and had previously spoken about the end with the Corinthians. He reminds them that they knew it, believed it, and chose to stand on it. You and I are readers of this truth, as well. We know the end. We believe in the end. We choose to stand on the end of Christ's life story.

Yes, Jesus died for our sins just as Scripture prophesied throughout the Old Testament and throughout the four Gospels. He died for you. He died on the cross in His perfect holiness clothed in our individual unrighteousness. He did this great sacrifice out of love deeper than anyone could ever demonstrate.

Friend, this is not what we stand on. We value and cherish His sacrifice. We sit in awe of His love. We struggle with fully grasping the weight He bore for each of us. We cannot even fathom Jesus. However, this is not what we stand on. This is the beginning. The beginning is good. It is astounding. But it is not the end-all on which we stand.

Oh, but consider that He spoke life over death, that He buried our rags of unrighteousness in the depth of eternity and clothed us in eternal robes of purity, that He destroyed the curse of the grave, that He rose again as prophesied throughout Scripture! This. This is the cornerstone on which we stand!

The Corinthian believers were struggling with belief in Christ's resurrection due to the philosophical stance of Corinth. According to Greek philosophy and Corinth's mythology, resurrection did not exist. Once gone, it is gone. Once dead, it is dead. There is no resurrection of life—neither is there a debate on this topic. It is a one-way street of philosophical agreement.

Imagine becoming a follower of Jesus as a resident of a mythically founded city, mythology being your philosophical truth. Then Jesus. Can you feel the raging battle within? Knowing resurrection does not exist, but also knowing that Jesus died and rose again. It is quite the contrary. Furthermore, this new knowledge was proving to be a quieted conversation among the Christian and the unsaved. They were keeping their newfound knowledge to themselves so as not to make waves with the unsaved of their community.

Scripture:

> *Now if Christ is proclaimed as raised from the dead,*
> *how can some of you say*
> *that there is no resurrection of the dead?*
> *But if there is no resurrection of the dead,*
> *then not even Christ has been raised.*
> *And if Christ has not been raised,*
> *then our preaching is in vain*
> *and your faith is in vain.*
> *If in Christ we have hope in this life only,*
> *we are of all people most to be pitied.*
> *For some have no knowledge of God.*
> *I say this to your shame.*
> *1 Corinthians 15:12–14, 19, 34b*

This makes me wonder about today. It makes me wonder what philosophical ideal is circulating around our society in which we silence our speech so as not to make waves. There is a fine line between being all for all men so that some will get saved from 1 Corinthians Chapter 10, and this mentality of standing up for our faith.

Just last night, my teenage son and I were watching debates on YouTube. Debates between theologian Ken Ham and TV personality Bill Nye. In one of these debates, Ham asked Nye what, if anything, would persuade him to change his mind about the existence of a Creator God.

"We would need just one piece of evidence, we would need the fossil that swam from one layer to another; we would need evidence that the universe is not expanding, we need evidence...Bring out any of those things, and you would change me immediately."[112] I found his deep desire for factual evidence at odds with itself. His stance shows an absence of factual evidence, yet he still believes in evolution.

The question in Corinth was like that of Bill Nye's. People were searching for factual evidence of a resurrected being.

Scripture:

> But someone will ask,
> "How are the dead raised?
> With what kind of body do they come?"
> You foolish person!
> What you sow does not come to life unless it dies.
> And what you sow is not the body that is to be,
> but a bare kernel,
> perhaps of wheat or of some other grain.
> But God gives it a body as he has chosen,
> and to each kind of seed its own body.
> 1 Corinthians 15:35–38

The answer to a philosophical root is Scriptural truth. God uproots evidential proof by His simple truth—if a seed of the acknowledgement

---

[112] Answers in Genesis. "Bill Nye Debates Ken Ham" February 4. 2014, Video, 2:38:12. Bill Nye Debates Ken Ham - HD (Official) - YouTube

of God exists. If God does not exist in the mind of the debater, then the issue of debate is futile. In this, I mean, you will rarely steer the heart of debaters to truth when they will not allow God on the table. The outcome of persuasion is minimal. However, if the conversation of philosophical differences arise, and you can get to the root issue (the existence of Jesus Christ), then fruit is feasible.

Jesus Christ is the answer to the question. Regardless as to what the question is. And, Friend, this is not blind faith. This is truth declared by God, written in His Word, lived out by Jesus Christ, and renewed within us by the washing of the Holy Spirit.

Jesus is factual, evidential truth.

Here is our takeaway: Debate with others when the opportunity to declare the name of Jesus Christ is present. Listen to debaters such as Ken Ham and Lee Strobel. These two men are efficient in what they do. They are passionate about their topics, for their topics point each debate to the solid proof of God — Jesus Christ.

However, if a conversation arises in which there is no ear for the name of Christ, then reread 1 Corinthians Chapter 10. Regain strength to simply listen to the argument at hand, engage in eye contact and facial response. Pray for words and for timing. And stay quiet until the Lord answers your prayers with the right words and the right timing. Do not ruin an opportunity to testify with your eagerness to prove God to be true.

God can handle a denier. He proved this when he sent Jesus.

How greatly I love that Paul gets personal at this point in the chapter! Sometimes, I think we get kerfuffled in debatable conversations because we are not solid in Scripture. I hear the hearts of many women who wish they knew more Scripture. Here is the beautiful thing with a heart's wish of a woman. She can. She can know more Scripture!

We may not know *all* Scripture, but we can know *more* Scripture. Furthermore, we can be confident in the Scripture that we know. We can be confident in the start of our Scripture knowledge because what we know is based on the Holy Spirit, and we are confident in Him. Does that make sense?

This personal passage recorded right here in 1 Corinthians 15 is a brilliant place to start.

Scripture:

> *For not all flesh is the same,*
> *but there is one kind for humans,*
> *another for animals,*
> *another for birds,*
> *and another for fish.*
> *There are heavenly bodies and earthly bodies,*
> *but the glory of the heavenly is of one kind,*
> *and the glory of the earthly is of another.*
> *There is one glory of the sun,*
> *and another glory of the moon,*
> *and another glory of the stars;*
> *for star differs from star in glory.*
> *1 Corinthians 15:39–41*

There is a tad bit of Dr. Seuss simplicity in this passage. A little bit of "red fish, blue fish" going on here. Do you see that? Paul opens the Corinthian eyes by painting a theatrical display of humans differing from animals in their designs.

Man dressed in top hat crosses from stage right as giraffe with bow tie bounds from the left.

Further he says, the flesh of a bird is different than the flesh of fish.

To learn that we do not have the same flesh as fish, nor do cows have a similarity with turkeys, is not a shocking revelation. It is common knowledge. Indisputable. It is in this same level of common knowledge that Paul points to the heavenly sphere. In this level of common knowledge, his connection makes a valid point.

There is a difference, he says, between an earthly body and a heavenly body. In other words, angels and men differ as greatly as the sun differs from the moon and as a star differs from a star.

Each creation from the hand of God is uniquely designed to withstand the elements in which it shines. Does this make sense? If so, let us bring these simple theatrics back to the heart of the matter: resurrection.

Scripture:

> *So is it with the resurrection of the dead.*
> *What is sown is perishable;*
> *what is raised is imperishable.*
> *It is sown in dishonor;*
> *it is raised in glory.*
> *It is sown in weakness;*
> *it is raised in power.*
> *It is sown a natural body;*
> *it is raised a spiritual body.*
> *If there is a natural body,*
> *there is also a spiritual body.*
> *1 Corinthians 15:42–44*

Remember, he wrote this chapter to a Christian body that resides within a Greek city. Remember also that the Greeks did not believe in resurrection. Therefore, these Christians were trying to testify about the death, burial, and resurrection of Jesus Christ to a nation that did not believe in resurrection at all.

The idea of Jesus conquering death could not resonate in this culture. So, Paul is giving them a written argument. I appreciate how he approaches the argument based on where the culture lies—in theatre and philosophy.

Paul lays it all on the table. First by referencing modern culture in verses 32 and 33. Then by staging a scene with poetic theatrics. Paul truly connected the hearts of the Corinthian Christians with the proper insight they needed to meet the Corinthians where they were. Brilliant. In this, he demonstrated the very heart of 1 Corinthians 9!

Lastly, he brings the conversation full circle.

An apple seed does not give a visual as to what its apple is going to look like. Nor does a pumpkin seed reveal its abundant orange shell. Every gardener knows that when you plant a seed, that seed must die before life resurrects from it. Every tree, plant and flower has bloomed in its creation upon the death of its natural seed.

Jesus willingly followed the example displayed by His very creation for His most cherished creation — you and me. He died as the seed of love and resurrected as the tree of life. Friend, we are the fruit from that tree. We are living abundantly in the gift of His love. Within us, He planted a seed that would one day die.

Scriptural Paraphrase:

The corpse that's planted is no beauty,
but when it's raised,
it's glorious.
Put in the ground weak,
it comes up powerful.
The seed sown is natural;
the seed grown is supernatural —
same seed, same body,
but what difference
from when it goes down in physical mortality
to when it is raised in spiritual immortality!
Eugene Peterson, The Message, verses 42–44

Think of the difference that occurred in your heart after you believed in the truth of Jesus Christ. Think about the transformation that happened in your mind and your thoughts after the presence of the Holy Spirit filled you. Habits changed within your desire. Your reputation began to shift in the eyes of those around you. Life became different than it was without Jesus. All these things are natural fruits springing forth from the spiritual seed planted within you.

Ultimately, the moment you believed in Jesus as the only way to truth and life, you died to yourself and rose again in the newness of Christ Jesus. It is our proclamation of this newness that we portray in baptism. We are agreeing with and identifying with the death, burial, and resurrection of our Savior.

In his book, *Be Wise*, Warren W. Wiersbe puts it this way, "If at the resurrection, all God did was to put us back together again, there would be no improvement. Furthermore, flesh and blood cannot inherit God's kingdom. The only way we can enjoy the glory of heaven is to have a body suited to that environment."[113]

If God has the power to resurrect our soul into the image of His Son, then what is stopping His power to resurrect our bodies into the image of our spiritual identity?

Scripture:

Thus it is written,
"The first man Adam became a living being";
the last Adam became a life-giving spirit.
But it is not the spiritual that is first
but the natural, and then the spiritual.
The first man was from the earth,
a man of dust;
the second man is from heaven.

As was the man of dust,
so also are those who are of the dust,
and as is the man of heaven,

---

[113] Warren W. Wiersbe, *Be Wise* (Colorado: David C. Cook, 1982), 170–171

> *so also are those who are of heaven.*
> *Just as we have borne the image of the man of dust,*
> *we shall also bear the image of the man of heaven.*
> *I tell you this, brothers:*
> *flesh and blood cannot inherit the kingdom of God,*
> *nor does the perishable inherit the imperishable.*
> *1 Corinthians 15:45–50*

Until that day in which we enter eternal life in Heaven, we are alive and present in our individual bodies, hand-crafted by the Creator, fit for the environment in which we live today. The question is, what are we doing with this seed of life? Are we taking full advantage of the fruit of the Spirit? Are we watering it, feeding it, and filling it with the light of the Lord? Our days on Earth are few. My prayer is that we will stand on truth gleaned in this study of 1 Corinthians and produce fruit fit for the Master's use.

Scripture:

> *Behold!*
> *I tell you a mystery.*
> *We shall not all sleep,*
> *but we shall all be changed,*
> *in a moment,*
> *in the twinkling of an eye,*
> *at the last trumpet.*
> *For the trumpet will sound,*
> *and the dead will be raised imperishable,*
> *and we shall be changed.*
> *1 Corinthians 15:51–52*

Some of us read that passage above with our gloves on. We see the debate of these verses. We tighten our gloves. We stand strong on our viewpoint. To us I say, "May we return to 1 Corinthians Chapter 1?"

Do you recall the divisions that were destroying the communion of the church of God? Do you remember the statement that settled it all? Did Jesus die for you? Yes! Did Jesus rise again for you? Yes.

Unity must ensue on that ground. Did you know there is room within the body of Christ for disagreement? Various convictions, thoughts, and matters of theological opinions differ. And that is okay — lest division follows. Lest we allow these differences to take our eyes off Jesus. When our eyes shift from Jesus to another's differing thoughts, we neglect the souls of men. How shameful it is when the unsaved see a visual argument within the heart of the Family of God!

How is this division beneficial to the Kingdom of God? Let me just be blunt. It is not. So, here is what we do. We respect one another in our viewpoints of eschatology (end times study) and remember that in the end, it is all about Jesus. One day, we will know who was right. But I have a feeling that when that day comes, we are not going to do a victory dance over being right. Rather, we will be free and alive to dance before the King of kings. I can only imagine.

Let us not cast judgment upon one another's differences in eschatology. Rather, let us declare the end. Jesus, our resurrected King, is coming again! Judgment easily vanishes when we declare the end in unison.

Scripture:

> *For this perishable body must put on the imperishable,*
> *and this mortal body must put on immortality.*
> *When the perishable puts on the imperishable,*
> *and the mortal puts on immortality,*
> *then shall come to pass the saying that is written:*
> *"Death is swallowed up in victory."* [114]
> *"O death, where is your victory?*
> *O death, where is your sting?"*
> *The sting of death is sin,*
> *and the power of sin is the law.*
> *But thanks be to God,*
> *who gives us the victory through our Lord Jesus Christ.*
> *1 Corinthians 15:53–57*

---

[114] Isaiah 25:8

This passage of glittered truth sparks a gleeful pause within our souls, doesn't it? It sums up the entirety of 1 Corinthians with simplistic promise. *"O death, where is your victory? O death, where is your sting?"* (v. 55) Christ's resurrection swallowed both the victory and the sting of death! Again, breathtakingly beautiful!

Sweet friend, if you are mourning the death of someone you hold dear, may I encourage you to sit with the sweet promise of our Savior? Death hurts. Emptiness remains. Life has lost its normal. And in the freshness of this heartache, we sit. And it is okay. Emotion is part of our design. It is okay to be emotional, to grieve and utilize the precious tear ducts God so graciously gave us. It is okay to be silent. Rest in the moment. Hope in the promise. Breathe in, breathe out.

Friend, remember the end! We have seen it spilled across the pages of our written Word of God penned by the precious blood of Jesus Christ. We know the end. Set your mind on the end.

It turns out, Judy's mentality is a jewel for us to behold, for when we know the end the rest of the story is easier to understand.

Not only is *His* end our comfort, but so is *our* end — in Him. That is the beautiful power of the resurrection promise!

Notes

1 Corinthians 16

Now concerning the collection for the saints: as I directed the churches of Galatia, so you also are to do. On the first day of every week, each of you is to put something aside and store it up, as he may prosper, so that there will be no collecting when I come. And when I arrive, I will send those whom you accredit by letter to carry your gift to Jerusalem. If it seems advisable that I should go also, they will accompany me.

I will visit you after passing through Macedonia, for I intend to pass through Macedonia, and perhaps I will stay with you or even spend the winter, so that you may help me on my journey, wherever I go. For I do not want to see you now just in passing. I hope to spend some time with you, if the Lord permits. But I will stay in Ephesus until Pentecost, for a wide door for effective work has opened to me, and there are many adversaries.

When Timothy comes, see that you put him at ease among you, for he is doing the work of the Lord, as I am. So let no one despise him. Help him on his way in peace, that he may return to me, for I am expecting him with the brothers.

Now concerning our brother Apollos, I strongly urged him to visit you with the other brothers, but it was not at all his will to come now. He will come when he has opportunity.

Be watchful, stand firm in the faith, act like men, be strong. Let all that you do be done in love.

Now I urge you, brothers — you know that the household of Stephanas were the first converts in Achaia, and that they have devoted themselves to the service of the saints — be subject to such as these, and to every fellow worker and laborer. I rejoice at the coming of Stephanas and Fortunatus and Achaicus, because they have made up for your absence, for they refreshed my spirit as well as yours. Give recognition to such people.

The churches of Asia send you greetings. Aquila and Prisca, together with the church in their house, send you hearty greetings in the Lord. All the brothers send you greetings. Greet one another with a holy kiss.

I, Paul, write this greeting with my own hand. If anyone has no love for the Lord, let him be accursed. Our Lord, come! The grace of the Lord Jesus be with you. My love be with you all in Christ Jesus. Amen.

16

Therefore, Live in Truth

Let all that you do be done in love.
1 Corinthians 16:14

And here we are sitting at the end of a deep, yet sweet, conversation. How are you doing? Seriously? I am a little shaky, a bit ready, and fully overcome with a whole new feeling of freedom. I pray that as we close our study in Paul fashion that we will unite in this freedom of judgment. May we live in our freedom found solely in the Word.[115] If you do not know where to begin this process of living free of improper judgment, then begin with one relationship. Pray over your judgment with that person, compare your judgment to the words found in 1 Corinthians — as if this letter is now your personal road map. Utilize what you have learned from Paul and practice, always. And when judgment comes, pause to match that judgment to this letter, as well. If it is positive judgment for your growth in Jesus Christ, then grow in Jesus Christ. If it is not Scriptural judgment, then proclaim your truths from Chapter 3 and grow in Jesus Christ. The greatest aspect of living free in Jesus is that we, both you and I, are now free to fully grow as the Spirit leads us to grow in the name of our Lord and Savior Jesus Christ.

---

[115] John 1:1

But we are not done. Not just yet. Paul tends to close his letters out with a final charge and with sweet salutations. I pray we will grab hold of his closing words in a truly applicable manner. Perhaps we will be led to emulate these words in our own lives. Pen, if you will, a final charge and sweet salutations to the ones we hold in upmost appreciation for their love for God.

Scripture:

> *Now concerning the collection for the saints:*
> *as I directed the churches of Galatia,*
> *so you also are to do.*
> *On the first day of every week,*
> *each of you is to put something aside and store it up,*
> *as he may prosper,*
> *so that there will be no collecting when I come.*
> *1 Corinthians 16:1–2*

First, Paul directs his final charge to the receivers of this letter. As modern-day hearers of these words, I charge you and me to heed these words well. And in our heeding, we must keep our eyes set on God above not on the hands of others. Catch what Paul is saying to these new Christians. On the first day of the week, you bring something as God gives to you.

Some of us struggle with the idea of giving tithes, giving to the church, or hearing anything that is directed at our personal finances. As we sit together in this study of judgment, let us purpose to step back and look at this charge with fresh eyes. The Corinthians had a question regarding their responsibility with this "collection of the saints" process. They wanted to know what that looked like and what their expected role was. These are all fair questions, and Paul answers them with simplicity.

Although we are not under a rule of law regarding giving in any fashion — it is not a New Testament command given by Jesus Christ — we are part of the body of Christ. We have seen what that looks like in Scripture, and many of us know what that feels like to be a part of this amazing family of God. And, really, that is all there is to say about our giving habits today. You are a member of this body, so *live* as if you are a member of the body.

Just as there are many members in the body, so are there many ways to give within the body. We cannot all give in the same manner. Whether it is a financial discussion, labor discussion, time discussion — whatever God has given you, give some of *that* to the Lord. Always, in your giving, give whatever it is to the Lord. No rules. No obligations. Simply you and what you have. Always with your eyes on Jesus, give.

Scripture:

> *And when I arrive,*
> *I will send those whom you accredit by letter*
> *to carry your gift to Jerusalem.*
> *If it seems advisable that I should go also,*
> *they will accompany me.*
> *I will visit you after passing through Macedonia,*
> *for I intend to pass through Macedonia,*
> *and perhaps I will stay with you*
> *or even spend the winter,*
> *so that you may help me on my journey,*
> *wherever I go.*
>
> *For I do not want to see you now just in passing.*
> *I hope to spend some time with you,*
> *if the Lord permits.*
> *But I will stay in Ephesus until Pentecost,*
> *for a wide door for effective work*
> *has opened to me,*
> *and there are many adversaries.*
> *1 Corinthians 16:3–9*

Paul's second charge is regarding himself. This is truly a precious section regarding sweet responses in place of ill-placed judgment. Here we see Paul's heart to be with his people, both in Corinth and in Ephesus.

His heart desires to be with both communities. And he knows that both want to have Paul with them.

Paul had to purpose to be present where he was, for "effective work" stood before him there in Ephesus and in that work—to fight the fight. I hear his words regarding the adversaries that stood against the work of the Lord, and I hear his final words to Timothy, "I have fought the good fight." [116]

In Paul's stay in Ephesus, a question mark loomed regarding when Paul's arrival in Corinth would occur. The delay is an open door for silly judgment. This happens so quickly within our hearts. A pastor or spiritual influence has a schedule shift, and we see it as a personal attack of our place in their heart. I do not know if this slight judgment of internal hurt occurred within the body of the Corinthians, nor do I know if you have ever felt this sorrow that led to a judgment of a respected and loved leader. I do know that I have seen this happen, and I know that I have been guilty of such a self-protective judgment as this.

May we, rather, pray over the people and their schedules. May we pray for their family and home matters, for their health and the well-being of their people. And may we see a bigger picture and understand that the work of the Holy Spirit may have allowed the delay or rescheduling. And in our determination to pray in place of judgment, let us press on in our service and love for our God.

Scripture:

When Timothy comes,
see that you put him at ease among you,
for he is doing the work of the Lord,
as I am.

So let no one despise him.
Help him on his way in peace,

---

[116] 2 Timothy 4:7

> *that he may return to me,*
> *for I am expecting him with the brothers.*
>
> *Now concerning our brother Apollos,*
> *I strongly urged him to visit you*
> *with the other brothers,*
> *but it was not at all his will to come now.*
> *He will come when he has opportunity.*
>
> *Be watchful,*
> *stand firm in the faith,*
> *act like men, be strong.*
> *Let all that you do be done in love.*
> *1 Corinthians 16:10–14*

Paul offers a charge regarding servants within the family of God. How sweet is the mention of others in 1 Corinthians Chapter 16 in contrast to Chapter 1. In fact, much of what Paul pens in this closing chapter is similar to his opening statements. They are beautiful chapters to read side by side. I encourage you to read these words together. I even deepen that challenge to reading this letter one more time allowing the truths of the Word to root within you that you may stand taller, declare your purpose with more surety, uphold Christ's presence in you with pure boldness, and fall in love with Jesus increasingly.

When the truths of the Word grow deeper within us, it frees our hearts to care for those around us. This is the heart of these last words. Give, he says, as God gives to you as you are and where you are. Care for those who come to you. See the individual and his/her needs. Fill others with what they are lacking whether it is joy, comfort, strength, or encouragement. As the Lord has given you in these areas, you are to give to them. He offers this charge about his own coming, for Timothy and for Apollos. Each situation and arrival are so different. With the wrong eyes, judgment could be cast upon each of these situations. But with the eyes of freedom in Christ, there is only love for these men and prayers poured over their travels, God's timing, and God's use for them.

At this moment, Paul offers a pointed exhortation. It is fascinating to see the timing of these five specific commands. In the midst of directing the Corinthians' eyes to a young servant and a well-respected servant, Timothy and Apollos, Paul says, "Be watchful." (v.13) It makes me ask why they are to be watchful? Deeper still, why are we to be watchful?

I declare, considering 1 Corinthians Chapters 1 and 15, that I firmly believe we are to care for those who serve, both the new in ministry and the rooted leadership, as we "wait for the revealing of our Lord Jesus Christ."[117]

Be watchful. Be watchful of all that we have gleaned from the words of Paul in this personal letter to a new body of believers. Oh, that our eyes will be set on the coming of the Lord, that our actions may benefit those who serve the Lord for our growth in Jesus!

Furthermore, Paul declares, "...stand firm in the faith." What a powerful exhortation for you and me today. Stand. Stand firm, grounded, rooted, established, and built up in the faith in which you have in God through the blood and resurrection of your Savior, Jesus Christ. Stand firm in that faith and that faith alone. Allow that faith to be the foundation on which you stand and work and serve and build up the church around you.

"Act like men" is a slightly comical charge for us to ponder as a body of women. But it is a charge for us to cling to, nonetheless. For this reason and this reason alone—God created man in the image of God Himself. It is in that boldness or that courage that Paul is encouraging each of us to act. Let us purpose to look at the faith of those who have acted like men, who were bold in their faith, and whose courage carried them into the Eternal Victory promised to all who believe in the name of Jesus Christ the Son of God.[118] Yes, let us carry that torch with a strong, victorious,

---

[117] 1 Corinthians 1:7
[118] Hebrews 11

Christian pride![119] And in your boldness, be strong. Shall we insert a mini study of Joshua at this point?

In fact, as this study ends, perhaps you will desire to take on a personal study of Hebrews 11. That one chapter offers an in-depth Scripture study of those who have gone before us in boldness and strength. Challenge yourself to use the stories listed in Hebrews 11 to direct you to the individual accounts detailed throughout the Old Testament. As you look up and read each account (slowly, intentionally, and with fresh eyes), take note of each man's actions of boldness and courage. Ask questions as you read. Write down the questions in your heart — even those big ones that seem impossible to answer. Then seek the answers to each of your questions as you read one more passage of Scripture — just you and God. It may surprise you, and it will grow you to see all that you glean from a personal Scripture study without the aide and guide of a Bible study book. Scripture is rich! The Spirit is within you! Read the precious Word of God and behold what wonderful things God has for you to seek and to find as you are and where you are today.

More than anything else, Paul concludes, remember that all God has done was and is in love; therefore, as one made in His image, do all that you do in love. Be watchful in love. Stand firm in love. Act in love. Demonstrate His strength in you in love. Also, love. For it is in our love for Him and for one another that the world will see Jesus and that the lost in this world will believe and follow our sweet Savior.[120]

Scripture:

> *Now I urge you, brothers —*
> *you know that the household of Stephanas*
> *were the first converts in Achaia,*
> *and that they have devoted themselves*
> *to the service of the saints —*
> *be subject to such as these,*

---

[119] Ephesians 6
[120] 1 John

and to every fellow worker and laborer.
I rejoice at the coming
of Stephanas and Fortunatus and Achaicus,
because they have made up for your absence,
for they refreshed my spirit as well as yours.

Give recognition to such people.
The churches of Asia send you greetings.
Aquila and Prisca, together
with the church in their house,
send you hearty greetings in the Lord.
All the brothers send you greetings.
Greet one another with a holy kiss.
1 Corinthians 16:15–20

Paul then mentions people lesser known to us but well known to this body of believers. Some are mentioned elsewhere in Scripture like Stephanas[121] and Aquila and Prisca (Priscilla);[122] others are only mentioned here like Fortunatus and Achaicus. Over each fellow worker and laborer, named or not, Paul washes a charge of submission and love upon them for their faithfulness to God in the body of Christ. Remembering not to elevate them to the point of division but considering their work as servants together in the Lord Jesus Christ.[123]

Who would make your list of fellow servants of the Lord? What a beautiful place to practice your personal journey of sharpened judgment. Begin with those with whom you are serving the Lord. Maybe, you do not have a list... I encourage you to start with that step and serve. Volunteer at your church. Serve in your body of Christ. Be engaged with the Christian family God has planted you in and near. Just start today. And then print the name or names of those beside whom you serve.

With our list of names, I challenge each of us to get on our knees in prayer over this list every day. Yes, on our knees and, yes, every day. The

---

[121] 1 Corinthians 1:16
[122] Romans 16:3; Acts 18; 2 Timothy 4:19
[123] 1 Corinthians 3

enemy is hungry to devour the fruit of your team. He often does this by causing dumb opportunities for judgment between us. If we remain faithful in praying for and with one another, we are defeating his cause before his attempt. Let us not slip in this power of prayer! The enemy is waiting for us to rely on our own strength in place of the power of prayer and of the Spirit. Oh, that we pour prayer over our team every day! Fight the good fight of faith together through prayer.

Scripture:

> *I, Paul, write this greeting with my own hand.*
> *If anyone has no love for the Lord,*
> *let him be accursed.*
> *Our Lord, come!*
> *The grace of the Lord Jesus be with you.*
> *My love be with you all in Christ Jesus.*
> *Amen.*
> *1 Corinthians 16:21–24*

Ah, Sweet Friend, will you stand? With your roots digging deep in the soil of God's love for you found in His Son, Jesus Christ, and with your roots nourished with the filling of the Holy Spirit in you and His gifts given you, will you stand? Stand tall on the truths of who you are in God. Stand tall on the truths of who you are in Christ Jesus. Stand tall on the truths of who you are in the Spirit of God. And give! Give freely of His love and through His gifts, so that the name of Jesus Christ can spread to one more heart. His love is contagious. Therefore, love.

As you stand in truth, use your tool of judgment according to Scripture so that division dares not overshadow the name of Jesus Christ. Allow the light of His love to spread for the growth of the body of Christ so that that the lost may be found. For those reasons, our precious Savior came, and for those reasons, we live. Therefore, live.

Thank you for reading *Stand in Truth*. More deeply, thank you for reading and studying 1 Corinthians. In the process of soaking in this letter, both your life and the lives of those around you will flourish in the freedom found simply by learning how to live in the freedom of judgment. My lasting prayer is that we will stand in God's truth. May we love and live as gold in the eyes of our God.

1 Corinthians 3:12
Jaclyn

Notes

Acknowledgments

Don and Peyton - What would I even do without my Everything and my Favorite Gift? How spoiled I am to be your wife and your mom. May God steal all the glory for all that we have in our home and in our hearts. I love you both.

Carolyn - You make me sound good. In other words, you, My Dear, are a miracle worker! Even with my fragments. *Insert giggle* Thank you for laying your gift before the Throne. How beautiful to see what God will do with our bits when they fall before Him! What a journey we had during this process, huh? Shall I say, what miracles we beheld during this journey! How great is our God?! May God receive all glory from our work!

Linda - You are so cool! I will forever throw this "accusation" at you! Because it is so true. It is a true joy to serve our Lord shoulder to shoulder with you. You—so cool, so professional. Me—not so much. Ha! Thank you for using your gift of design and professionalism in the finalizing of this book. The book cover is lovely. Thank you for your part in editing, detailing, and finalizing its beauty.

Kelly - We've done a *couple of things* together—as girlfriends and as co-servants of Christ. And now we can add "Write & Proofread a non-fiction book" to that beautiful list. Here's to all those years of painting our nails, teaching Scripture and giggling…together! I love God's gift of our friendship. I love you. You, too, Fred. Thank you for your faithfulness to Bible knowledge. Thank you for your "brotherness" in my heart.

Readers - Different phases; different readers. *Stand in Truth* has been held in prayer and active participation by so many amazing hearts! This book started in a binder with the title, *Judged Not*. That year, with my DHCP study group, produced the fruit of what is published today. Truly, thank you for that time spent together. Then there are the permission readers: namely, my wonderful mother-in-law per Chapter 15. And, finally, my completion readers: Gail, Rhiannon, Lisa, Kelly, and Don whose eyes and insight brought the smallest of details to a shining light. From the depths of my little toe, thank you! Abundantly!

Prayer warriors - To list the hearts who have held and are continuing to hold *Stand in Truth* in prayer would be too vast of a list—a truth that overwhelms my heart! From my Glitter Warriors to my Women Inseparable, from my sister in Florida to my best friend in Togo. This book and its author have been so lovingly laid before the Throne of God. How does one even begin to say Thank you to such a grand gift?

> *I do not cease to give thanks for you, remembering you in my prayers,*
> *that the God of our Lord Jesus Christ, the Father of glory,*
> *may give you the Spirit of wisdom and of revelation*
> *in the knowledge of him,*
> *having the eyes of your hearts enlightened,*
> *that you may know what is the hope to which he has called you,*
> *–Ephesians 1:16–18a*

Jesus - I sit in awe at your feet, surrounded by my family, my friends, and my Women Inseparable to say Thank You for giving us the gift of the Bible. This tangible gift, Lord Jesus, is everything to us. Selah. How great and how mighty You are, the Word from the beginning. The very Son of God who was and who is and who is to come. No height, no depth, nothing can change who You are. Nothing can change Your love for us. And. Jesus, nothing can change our status as "Yours" because of the sovereignty, surety, and steadfastness of Your love. Oh, how great and how mighty You are, Lord Jesus! May we worship You! May we give You praise! May our lives be to You a pleasing aroma that, as Paul declares, some may be saved. This is my prayer. Thank You for entrusting us with the gift of Your Word, the Spirit of our God, and the opportunity to be the Light of the world.

We are for You,
Amen

About the Book

The Painting - After teaching week three of our Women Inseparable study, *Who Holds Forgiveness*, I came home empty from all that was expressed during my teaching, yet I was full of the truth of God's imminent power over sin. In a state of silence and awe, I sat with my acrylics and a blank canvas. What formed from my heart to my paintbrush was a visual of God's path from one way of living to His presence in one's life.

I am far removed from the classification of "professional artist." However, I am in love with how God can use an ill-trained hand to produce something creative if only we are willing to paint, to write, to teach, to give, to sow, to reap…. That's all this cover is—a heart of gold with the touch of the Master's Hand.

The Digitalization - By my friend, Dandy Everist of *justDandy* photos. Follow her on Instagram @justdandy_photos. Schedule or purchase her designs at justdandyllc.com. Romans 5:1-5

About the Author

A Personal Note

Hi, I am Jaclyn Palmer. You learned a tad bit about me as you read this book but perhaps not too much. For this book was about the book of 1 Corinthians, and 1 Corinthians is about God's story. My prayer is that as you read this book and learned about Paul's letter to the Corinthian believers, you learned God's story enough that you will proclaim His story to those around you.

1 Corinthians was never on my top ten favorite books of the Bible list. It was never on my top one hundred list. Because there are only sixty-six books in the whole Bible, that's not exceptionally good odds.

God said to me, "*I want you to author a book on 1 Corinthians.*" And I said to God, "*No.*" This conversation continued for about a year before I humbly told God, "*Fine. I will read your book, but that is it.*" In reading a book I avidly avoided throughout my life, I found myself learning more about God's story and less about my apprehension toward Paul. After reading the book repeatedly, I learned more about my story and less about my judgers and judgments on others. I saw the missing pieces that we gather as stones of judgment. As I finally sat with my laptop and my open Bible, I began seeing the stones that I viewed as a form of protection lying at my feet. Stones of judgment that others have thrown at me found their way among the heap on my wood floor.

The freer my hands became, the greater was my desire to take in all that was suddenly new to my eyes, my heart, and my mind. I began a new journey in learning Scripture as if I had never read it before. This is my heart's desire for you. I pray that stones of judgment will fall steadily from your grip so that your heart may flourish in the goodness of God's love.

I would be honored to invite you to join me and women all around the world in declaring that we are Women Inseparable. Romans 8 tells us that nothing can separate us from the love of God that is in Christ Jesus our Lord. Nothing. As Women Inseparable, we know and live out our love for Him according to Scripture — as we are, where we are. It's sweet. It's real. And it is a consuming fire! Jesus desires that we do not lose our first love. May we together declare and live out our love for God that is in Christ Jesus our Lord! You are welcome to stand with us as is best for you. We study Scripture, pray, and laugh together during our live weekly studies. These studies are shared via podcast, video, and social media. Wherever you are, there is a place for you in Women Inseparable. xo

For more information visit

womeninseparable.com

Jaclyn Palmer

Made in the USA
Middletown, DE
13 April 2023